Nudging Democratized
A Guide to Applying Behavioral Science

Steve Shu & Andrew Lewis

Nudging Democratized: Copyright © 2019 by The Decision Lab

Inside Nudging: Copyright © 2016, 2019 by Steve Shu

All rights reserved. No part of this book may be reproduced in any form by any electronic or mechanical means (including photocopying, recording, or information storage and retrieval) without permission in writing from the copyright holders.

CONTENTS

Nudging, Democratized ... 1

Inside Nudging: Implementing Behavioral Science Initiatives ... 17

1 Behavioral Science Centered Design is the New Black ... 21

2 Organizations Can Package Behavioral Science for Good ... 35

3 Learn from Project-Based Approaches and Leverage Consulting Organizations ... 49

4 Look at Problems Holistically and Build an Innovation Capability ... 65

5 Nudge Psyche and Exploring Ethics ... 83

6 Inside Research and Testing ... 105

7 Nudging to Democratizing Outcomes ... 127

Acknowledgements ... 135

Bibliography ... 137

Appendix A: Ideas to Introduce Behavioral Science Initiatives ... 145

About the Author ... 159

NUDGING, DEMOCRATIZED

When the economist Herb Simon delivered his Nobel Prize lecture in 1979, he spoke with concern. Taking stock of the field, he worried it had become consumed with elegant but overly-simplified abstractions (models) of economic behavior, while ignoring how people *actually behave*. Meanwhile, the small strain of decision-based research that existed was upending some of the core assumptions of those models. Simon urged his colleagues to branch out: "the Heartland is more overpopulated than ever, while rich lands in other parts of the empire go untended."

Simon's own work on bounded rationality[1] had already knocked over the first pillar in the neoclassical house of cards that is *rational choice theory*. It showed how individual behavior systematically strays from standard economics' assumption of rationality; in fact, people do *not* have clearly defined and consistent preferences and do *not* always act to satisfy these

---

[1] Simon's bounded rationality was the first formal demonstration of how individual behavior systematically strays from the rational choice model. Limited by time, cognitive functioning, and motivation, bounded rationality demonstrated that — rather than considering all available information and arriving at the absolute *best* decision — people are willing to *satisfice* (a portmanteau of satisfy and suffice, meaning to accept a *pretty good* decision that is easier to arrive at).

preferences. At the time, nearly all economic theory was based on rational choice. Thus, as new research chipped away at the validity of this assumption, so too were the models becoming ineffective.

Quoting Alfred Marshall, himself a pioneer of neoclassical economics, Simon urged his colleagues to step back and remember that economics is "a psychological science." If one accepts this as true, how could economists pay so little attention to how people think and behave?

The standard response from Simon's peers was best summed up by Milton Friedman, who argued that models should be judged by whether their predictions are "good enough for the purpose in hand or…better than predictions from alternative theories." Perhaps that is so, Simon rebutted from the Nobel stage, but the standard model of economic behavior could not "provide a good prediction — not even a good approximation — of actual behavior."

Some forty years later, Simon's words ring true. In the decades since, a host of psychologically-informed research into human behavior has emerged, tending the far-flung acreage of the *economic kingdom*. Boasting a colorful array of names (organizational behavior, decision theory, management science, social psychology, behavioral and experimental economics), insights from these disciplines can more or less be bundled under the blanket header: behavioral science.

What We Talk About When We Talk About Behavioral Science

At the heart of this research are individuals, ourselves. How do we make the thousands of daily decisions that set the course of our lives? Do we do so with intention, in alignment with higher-order goals — or do we do so automatically, at the whim of some internal autopilot? What external conditions engender either mode of thinking? Indeed, how much are our decisions the results of our choice environments?

These are some of the central questions behavioral science seeks to answer. In describing our decision-making processes, the ultimate goal is to improve our decisions. Milton Friedman was right, the discipline has yet to produce — and likely will not produce — a single model of behavior that fits universally across individuals and contexts. It has, however, dramatically advanced our understanding of human decision-making.

Sometimes the insights gained from academic and scientific discovery are so profound as to change the way we understand, and operate in, the world around us. Once found, they afford all of us an understanding of the world that is, in a sense, more accurate than that of even the most learned person from generations past. Though it was, relatively speaking, a recent discovery, it is hard to imagine not knowing the sun is the center of our solar system. Nor is it easy to imagine our modern lives without things like electricity, or penicillin.

Yet, the theories and technologies that most advance humanity's collective knowledge are often too complex for the average person to engage with. While the theory of general relativity — often described as the most important scientific discovery in history — allows me to, for example, use my phone's GPS to navigate any part of the world without getting lost, I (and perhaps you) would be hard-pressed to offer much more than a rudimentary understanding of what it says.

Behavioral science is not like that. Its most fundamental insights — bounded rationality, time-discounting, prospect theory, heuristic decision-making, among others — often elicit something like an *"of course!"* from those to whom these insights are explained. It will surprise no one that we are prone to sub-optimal or not-fully-reasoned behaviors. And yet, though it strikes people as obvious that we might (consciously or subconsciously) care more about the present than the future, we still allow ourselves to make short-sighted decisions without accounting for our myopia.

When it comes to physical ailments, we address them without delay. People with actual myopia get eyeglasses to address the problem. Why not take a similar approach with our systematic behavioral errors? Often we already know, or at least sense, what these may be. The trick is to document them, and design environments in which they are least likely to negatively affect us. Behavioral science offers us the means to do this, and as such a toolkit for improving our decisions.

It is the comprehensibility of behavioral science insights that make it a field ripe for democratization. Too often the greatest advancements of our collective knowledge —

regarding the world, or ourselves — remain confined to a small group of highly-specialized academics. Sitting in pay-walled journals, jargon-laden and complex, they are beyond both our reach and understanding. With behavioral science this need not and should not be the case. Its insights into human behavior are perceptible to experts and laypeople alike, and equipped with such an understanding, we can endeavor to make simple changes to our decision-making contexts that tangibly change our behaviors and get us closer to the outcomes we desire.

These simple tweaks can be used, for example, by national governments to improve the collection of taxes, to the tune of millions of taxpayers' dollars saved; by health organizations to encourage people to keep up with their prescription medications, saving thousands of lives; or by you, to better align your behavior today with your goals for tomorrow. Such is the purpose of this book: to share the insights from and applications of behavioral science that we have found most useful, and believe can be applied by practitioners at low cost and with relative ease.

Nudging into the Mainstream

While the academic wheels of behavioral science kept turning after Simon's Nobel win, the last decade has seen the discipline propelled into the public consciousness. Much of this attention is thanks to the wave of non-academic publications written with the explicit intention of explaining behavioral science to a lay audience — in particular the enormously popular *Nudge*, in which authors Richard Thaler and Cass Sunstein detail the subtle ways our behavior can be, and is, manipulated by our environments. In turn, the word "nudge" has entered the common vernacular (to the tune of thousands of articles about how to nudge ourselves – or others – toward various goals), as has talk of the heuristics and biases that shape our decision processes.

Beyond gaining popular currency, behavioral science has also migrated from the halls of academia to the seats of international power. In 2010, the UK launched its much-lauded *"Nudge Unit"* (formally titled the Behavioural Insights Team, or BIT), at the behest of then-Prime Minister David Cameron. The unit came with an explicit mandate: wield knowledge of human behavior to improve the efficacy and efficiency of governmental programs — or, as it was put at the time, to do "more with less." Indeed, when properly applied, this is the hallmark of behavioral interventions: they make better use of resources.

For example, consider one of BIT's first and best-known projects (discussed in Chapter 1). Working with HMRC (the UK's tax collection agency), the unit was tasked with improving tax compliance, targeting those with delinquent payments. Whereas a traditional policy approach might have added an additional fee for non-compliance, or considered a shift in the collection strategy altogether, BIT's suggestion was exceedingly simple: play on people's desire to fit in. Using the same mail-based collection strategy as ever, the team added only a single line to the envelopes they sent out, telling people the percent of their neighbors who had paid their tax on time. The results were stunning: including this simple, and costless, piece of information increased payment rates by more than 5% within a month of the letters being sent, and overall led to an increase of GBP 210 million in taxes collected in the year 2012–2013 (Hallsworth et al, 2014).

This is the added value of behavioral science initiatives: to place *people*, and the (often predictable) ways we act, at the center of design. As nudge theory tells us, every decision happens within a *choice environment*[2], whether or not this is explicitly recognized. Too often, well-intentioned and promising policy or business initiatives are subverted by inattention to this crucial detail.

For example, consider how the placement of items in a cafeteria might affect your decision about what to eat. Imagine you've gathered your entree, and are progressing down a line toward the checkout counter. You want something else to complement your meal, but aren't sure what. If the next station offers dessert, perhaps you'll indulge. If, however, the next station offers fruit — and the desserts are all the way at the

---

[2] Put simply, a choice environment is any context in which we make decisions. When shopping for a sweater, the layout of the aisles, the temperature of the store, and whether credit cards are accepted could all affect our ultimate decision.

other side of the room — perhaps you'll stick with something healthy. This simple notion that our choices result in part from availability and convenience is the basis of numerous successful public health interventions. These studies find that, when more healthful options are made more convenient and less healthful options are made less convenient, people on average choose healthier foods (see, for example, Hanks et al, 2012).

Choice environments and nudge theory show us how much environmental cues matter. And, whether or not they have been explicitly designed to do so, they already affect our decisions. If that dessert had been next to the entrees, we would have taken it — meaning a default option already existed. Whether it was put there mindlessly or intentionally, the reality is we always exist in some choice environment or another, and these always suggest certain options as the easiest defaults. Thus, we can either proactively shape the forces that will affect us, or leave these forces to chance. The weight of empirical evidence has shown the latter comes at a high cost.

Nudging Towards Formalized Labor

Like the proper execution of a good recipe, the taste of BIT's success whet appetites for similar initiatives in governments the world across. In less than a decade since its 2010 launch, more than 200 similar public-sector programs have sprung up from Perth to Peru (eMBed, 2018). These units are using behavioral science to increase the efficacy of their existing policy initiatives, and the wide variety of contexts in which these groups now (successfully) operate bears testament to the universal value of paying attention to how people act.

Consider, for example, a recent intervention designed at the Mexican Ministry of Finance.[3] In Mexico, informal businesses employ around 30 million workers, or roughly a third of its working-age population — translating to a great sum of lost tax revenue. Further, employees of these informal businesses are ineligible to access social security benefits, as they are not officially listed on any payrolls. Thus, widespread informal labor constitutes a problem not just for the government's

---

[3] (BIT London, 2017)

coffers, but also for workers' wellbeing. As the country modernizes its economy, the government is determined to bring these businesses and workers out from the shadows.

To incentivize businesses to join the formal economy, the government offers significant tax discounts. Once a company formalizes, it is required to report its revenues and enroll its employees for social security benefits in order to receive those discounts. Thus, the policy is premised on traditional economic thinking: by providing a great enough monetary incentive, businesses will find it in their best interest to join the formal economy. And yet, to the government's dismay, far fewer businesses were joining the program and complying with its responsibilities — disqualifying them from the discounts, leaving their revenues uncollected, and keeping their employees out of social benefits systems.

In standard economic thinking, where actors are fully rational and have perfect access to and understanding of all the relevant information, non-compliance would indicate the businesses had considered the benefits of the discounts and actively decided to exit the program. Thus, the next step for such a policy would often be to inflict some punitive damage on the non-compliers. But what if there was another, simpler answer? What if a small nudge in the right direction could bring businesses back into compliance?

With the help of relevant Mexican agencies, the group set up an SMS program to send three types of reminders to delinquent businesses. And, knowing that the framing of a choice impacts significantly on how people respond, they tested messages with three different emphases:

1) *Deterrence*, highlighting "negative consequences of non-compliance";
2) *Reciprocity* reminding "taxpayers of the subsidies provided"; and
3) *Ease* providing "instructions on how to declare"

Each of these messages exploits a different insight into behavior. Deterrence plays on the axiom that *the pain of loss is greater than the pleasure of gain* (i.e., loss aversion): rather than touting the **benefits** of complying (e.g., you will continue to receive a substantial tax discount), they underscore the **loss** of benefits that noncompliance entails (e.g., you will lose the tax discount to which you are entitled).

Like the HRMC letter in the UK, the reciprocity message in Mexico plays on people's inherent preference toward *fairness* — our desire to treat people how they treat us. For more than a century economics (and by extension public policy) has premised its theories on *homo economicus*, a shrewd and singularly self-interested caricature of a human being always out for himself. But experiments on reciprocal behavior, such as those conducted by the economists Fehr and Gächter (2000), demonstrate that "in response to friendly actions, people are frequently much nicer and much more cooperative than predicted by the self-interest model; conversely, in response to hostile actions they are frequently much more nasty and even brutal." Said another way, we are driven by more than just monetary self-interest. Social interactions matter, environments matter, and both impact on the ways we behave.

Finally, the last message (ease) aims to make the process seem less daunting. Put simply, when we perceive a task to be complex — and therefore expect it will demand both time and cognitive resources — we are less likely to try and complete it. Sometimes called *burdened non-compliance*, this phenomenon is particularly acute in medicine, where complicated treatment regimens can lead people to stop taking their medications altogether, despite recognizing the benefits of following the prescribed regimen (see, for example, de Vries et al, 2014). Such is the basis for a wide range of behavioral public health interventions that use SMS reminders to help people navigate complicated treatments. A meta-analysis of these studies published in the Journal of the American Medical Association (JAMA) found that "mobile phone text messaging approximately doubles the odds of medication adherence" (Thakkar et al, 2016). Understanding that people are limited by finite cognitive and memory resources, and designing health treatments with this in mind, can quite literally save lives.

At this point, it will not surprise you that all three messages employed in Mexico led to a significant increase in businesses' rates of reporting, with the deterrence message increasing reporting rates by 37% compared to receiving no message at all. The whole program brought in 400% more revenue than it cost — despite the fact that most businesses received discounts of between 90 and 100% of their tax obligation. These simple, low-cost tweaks make policy more effective, and we all benefit from their doing so.

Nudging Towards Cleaner Air

Research conducted here at *The Decision Lab* (TDL) similarly emphasizes the importance of individual perceptions — and therefore the crucial role of framing — for how we respond to technological and policy change. Working with the World Bank, TDL was enlisted to help increase the use of efficient and environmentally friendly cookstoves in Uganda. In less-developed contexts across the world, households tend to rely on open fire stoves for cooking and heating their homes. In addition to being inefficient, these fires are highly toxic. According to Berkeley public health professor Kurt R. Smith, the smoke that comes from burning an average wood cookfire for one hour is equivalent to burning 300 cigarettes (Naeher et al, 2007).

The environmental and public health implications are even more dire: in 2012, the Global Burden of Disease study estimated some 3.5 million people die each year from respiratory illnesses resulting from exposure to household air pollution — more than the number of annual deaths attributed to malaria and HIV/AIDS combined (Wang et al, 2017). They are also highly inefficient, costing an estimated $50 billion per year in Africa alone. Of course, a number of safer and more efficient alternatives exist, many for less than $10. Thus, the Bank's task was simple: get people to use covered cookstoves.

At the time of the project only about 5% of Ugandans had adopted these new alternatives. In order to increase uptake, the Bank and other para-governmental institutions had previously focused on stressing the health benefits of switching. Yet, this strategy was failing to convince Ugandans to buy the new cookstoves. The dominant problem was perceptual: because the open, solid-burning cookstoves were the norm, new alternatives were viewed as a luxury. Health implications aside, it was difficult for households to justify to themselves "investing" in a new luxury good, whatever the price. Yet because these alternatives require less fuel, they actually increase disposable income in the long-run by roughly 20%. In other words, inefficient cookstoves are the luxury good: they cost more to use. In order to increase uptake, this point needed to be stressed.

Experimental evidence on the matter was clear: messaging that framed the old cookstove as a luxury item and the alternative as the more economical option significantly increased people's propensity to buy a new stove. Everything else aside, Ugandans were simply trying to use their financial resources as best they could — so this was the benefit of the new stoves that needed to be stressed. Here is another critical insight from behavioral science: before designing a policy, first understand the priorities of the people it will serve.

Nudging in the Private Sector

Outside the policy arena, private organizations are increasingly turning to behavioral scientists to help understand their employees and customers. Indeed, one of the most successful behavioral interventions to date was undertaken by the Nobel-winning economist Richard Thaler in conjunction with a number of private businesses of varying sizes. Worried that their employees were not saving adequately for retirement, they wondered if behavioral insights might be leveraged to encourage people to put more of their wages into savings accounts.

There are a number of barriers to saving money (including limited financial resources), but perhaps the greatest is what behavioral economists call *hyperbolic discounting* or *present bias*. Put simply, we place more value on the present relative to the future. In a famous demonstration, participants opted to take $1 in the present over $3 the following day (Thaler, 1981). As the "hyperbolic" moniker indicates, this effect compounds rapidly in the near-term, then slows in the long-term. For example, we will place a much greater value on the present relative to tomorrow or, say, a month in the future — but may not distinguish much between a month and five weeks.

Thus, convincing ourselves to save for retirement — that distant, almost mythical event we are told will someday come

— is decidedly unsatisfying in the present moment. Understanding this phenomenon, Thaler and the behavioral economist Shlomo Benartzi designed the Save More Tomorrow (SMarT) program to overcome the behavioral barriers to saving (discussed further in Chapter 2). Rather than ask employees to contribute in the present, they instead had them commit to saving a designated percentage of any future wage increases. By pulling from wages that will be gained in the future, they overcome two key impediments. First, present bias leads employees to discount the future value of their financial security in retirement; the SMarT program taps into that bias because the employees discount the future value of their contributions as well. Second, loss aversion makes it challenging for employees to make sacrifices from the standard of living they already have in order to save for later; the SMarT program increases retirement contributions when employees get a raise — so they will receive only a smaller gain in future, but never perceive a loss to what they already have.

The results showed this method to be an astounding success: 78% of employees offered the SMarT plan enrolled, 80% of those who enrolled remained, and the average savings rate increased almost fourfold from 3.5% to 13.6% over 40 months of observation (Thaler & Benartzi, 2004). By simply employing knowledge of human psychology, employers achieved a notoriously difficult feat: getting people to care about the future!

Since its initial rollout, the SMarT program has been implemented by countless private and public-sector employers. According to Benartzi's website, some 15 million Americans are enrolled in a SMarT savings program — and the Pension Protection Act of 2006 officially encouraged companies to employ the underlying method. By simply following the SMarT playbook, organizations large and small — from the federal government to family-run businesses — have improved their employees' futures, and in turn helped to mitigate the looming crisis of non-savings and financial insecurity among seniors.

Democratization

This is why behavioral science is ripe for democratization. But what does it mean to "democratize" behavioral science?

Here at The Decision Lab, we see two key components that define this democratization. First, these insights have to be *widely available* so that they can be applied. Like most areas of research, application of behavioral science is not an off-the-shelf deployment; rather, it is a process of contouring this knowledge into the proper shape as it is translated from the lab bench to the wider world of practice. In behavioral science, the gap is wide between the state of knowledge within the academic sphere and the state of practice beyond. A key component of our mission at The Decision Lab, therefore, is to ease the diffusion of that knowledge—to help close the gap.

Second, democratization means that putting behavioral science into practice has to be *responsible*. One of the core takeaways from behavioral science research is that our minds seldom operate in the way that we think they do; many things influence our decisions without us being aware that they are doing so—even without us being consciously aware that they are there. As a result, manipulating these factors can be used to covertly manipulate our decisions. Behavioral science that is truly democratized respects the dignity and the agency of people, it does not use them strictly as a means to an end. Accordingly, a second key component of our mission at The Decision Lab is to respect dignity and agency in the application of behavioral science: articulating the challenges one might encounter in applying behavioral science responsibly, outlining potential solutions to address these challenges, and helping the community of practitioners to act responsibly.

Conceiving of and properly testing a customized intervention in situ often requires expert knowledge and considerable resources. (There is a reason, after all, that firms such as The Decision Lab offer professional services in this domain.) However, there are also many general insights and broadly applicable interventions—several between the covers of this very book—that organizations can learn from and adopt even without guidance from a team of professionals. Moreover, individual- and firm-level changes ripple out to improve society at large. These accessible insights and low-cost solutions mean that any individual or organization can incorporate behavioral science into their toolkit. Taken from years of hands-on experience, the chapters that follow provide a practical guide to doing this: applying insights from behavioral science, widely and responsibly, to improve outcomes for society at large.

Andrew Lewis
July 2019

Works Cited

BIT, London. (2017). The Behavioural Insights Team Update Report 2016–17.

de Vries, S. T., Keers, J. C., Visser, R., de Zeeuw, D., Haaijer-Ruskamp, F. M., Voorham, J., & Denig, P. (2014). Medication beliefs, treatment complexity, and non-adherence to different drug classes in patients with type 2 diabetes. *Journal of Psychosomatic Research, 76*(2), 134-138.

Fehr, E., & Gächter, S. (2000). Fairness and retaliation: The economics of reciprocity. *Journal of Economic Perspectives, 14*(3), 159-181.

Friedman, M. (1953). The Methodology of Positive Economics, in *Essays in Positive Economics*. Chicago, Illinois: University of Chicago Press.

Hallsworth, M., Halpern, D., Algate, F., Gallagher, R., Nguyen, S., Ruda, S., ... & Reinhard, J. (2014). EAST Four simple ways to apply behavioural insights. *The Behavioural Insights Team Publications, Cabinet Office.*

Hanks, A. S., Just, D. R., Smith, L. E., & Wansink, B. (2012). Healthy convenience: nudging students toward healthier choices in the lunchroom. *Journal of Public Health, 34*(3), 370-376.

Martin, W. J., Glass, R. I., Balbus, J. M., & Collins, F. S. (2011). A major environmental cause of death. *Science, 334*(6053), 180-181.

Naeher, L. P., Brauer, M., Lipsett, M., Zelikoff, J. T., Simpson, C. D., Koenig, J. Q., & Smith, K. R. (2007). Woodsmoke health effects: a review. *Inhalation toxicology, 19*(1), 67-106.

Simon, H. A. (1979). Rational Decision Making in Business Organizations. *The American Economic Review, 69*(4), 493-513.

Thakkar, J., Kurup, R., Laba, T. L., Santo, K., Thiagalingam, A., Rodgers, A., ... & Chow, C. K. (2016). Mobile telephone text messaging for medication adherence in chronic disease: a meta-analysis. *JAMA Internal Medicine, 176*(3), 340-349.

Thaler, R. (1981). Some empirical evidence on dynamic inconsistency. *Economics Letters, 8*(3), 201-207.

Thaler, R. H., & Benartzi, S. (2004). Save more tomorrow™: Using behavioral economics to increase employee saving. *Journal of Political Economy, 112*(S1), S164-S187.

Wang, H., Abajobir, A. A., Abate, K. H., Abbafati, C., Abbas, K. M., Abd-Allah, F., ... & Adedeji, I. A. (2017). Global, regional, and national under-5 mortality, adult mortality, age-specific mortality, and life expectancy, 1970–2016: a systematic analysis for the Global Burden of Disease Study 2016. *The Lancet, 390*(10100), 1084-1150.

Inside Nudging
Implementing Behavioral Science Initiatives

Steve Shu

INSIDE NUDGING: IMPLEMENTING BEHAVIORAL SCIENCE INITIATIVES

My gut tells me that a gene exists that predisposes someone to startup situations. My father surely has it. With a partner, he started an innovative company that designed new computer chips, audio technologies, specialized circuits for analyzing blood, and computer graphics languages, just to name a few things. During my pre-teen to teenage years, I used to go into his office and interact with all types of people, including PhDs, engineers, crazy inventors, ex-game designers from Bally-Midway, and the like. My dad had coin-op video games in the office that I loved, like Spy Hunter and Defender. He also had some more obscure games like Professor Pac-Man and Pac-Man pinball. Some of my earliest memories at his office with hands-on technology included me using a proprietary computer graphics language to create visual demos like an animated Pac-Man and a three-dimensional spinning coin. It was quite a technology feat for the early eighties given that personal computers were relatively scarce. My dad also involved me by exposing me to business plans and pitches to angel investors. Collectively, those early experiences surely helped nurture my instincts around creating things, working in startup environments, and incubating new initiatives.

Fast-forward to the late nineties, after getting degrees in electrical engineering from Cornell University and spending five to six years as a nut-and-bolts engineer designing things, I attended the business school at The University of Chicago, and took a class, called Managerial Decision Making, which was taught by Professor Christopher Hsee. The very first paper in the course packet was "Judgment under Uncertainty: Heuristics and Biases" by Amos Tversky and Daniel Kahneman (Tversky and Kahneman, Judgment under Uncertainty: Heuristics and Biases 1974), a famous paper in the behavioral science area. Inside the classroom, I would get exposed to many other behavioral science concepts like loss aversion, where "losses loom larger than gains." In other words, losses really hurt; people experience losses two to two-and-a-half times as strongly as gains. In those years, I also got schooled in behavioral sciences outside of the classroom. One clever tactic that PRTM Management Consultants used on me was a shrinking bonus that made losses feel very proximate and self-inflicted. If I signed on right away to join the firm I would get an amount of money that would immediately pay for one full year of business school. Of course I had the option to delay signing with the firm. For every month that I delayed, the sign-on bonus would shrink by thousands of dollars. Steve, meet an intensely personal version of Loss Aversion!

So I wound up joining PRTM Management Consultants and started to hone my business strategy, leadership, and implementation skills. Over the years my background has heavily included experiences with new initiatives within larger companies. For example, I have been involved with incubating new groups or innovation projects within companies like Allscripts, Nortel, and Allianz Global Investors (with its Center for Behavioral Finance, where I have been a core member of the team since it was started in 2009).

In the past seven years or so, I have been involved with an increasing number of behavioral science projects. I use the term behavioral science to include cross-functional topics and disciplines like behavioral economics, behavioral finance, and psychology as popularized in books like *Nudge* (Thaler and Sunstein 2008), *Predictably Irrational* (Ariely 2010), or *Thinking, Fast and Slow* (Kahneman 2013). The upshot is that these books have really helped to raise awareness of behavioral science, which has in turn increased the number of opportunities I see. Additionally, as the world becomes increasingly digitalized, there has been an increasing amount of technology available to use in implementing behavioral science ideas. For example, my involvement with technology and behavioral science have included helping incubate new digital product offerings and strategic changes to enterprise business systems and websites. At a more tactical level, I've also helped to facilitate the development of portable and mobile applications, like the Retirement Goal Planning System by Allianz Global Investors (Allianz Global Investors Center for Behavioral Finance 2015) and the Loss Aversion Calculator by Digitai (Digitai n.d.).

Because the opportunities to apply behavioral science are increasing, I wanted to help people capitalize on those opportunities. I wrote *Inside Nudging* for management professionals and scientists to feed their thinking and discussions about implementing behavioral science initiatives (which includes behavioral economics and finance) in business settings. Situations include the incubation of innovation centers, behavioral science overlay capabilities, and advancement of existing organizations. Companies need to develop grit - the ability and fortitude to succeed. The book introduces the Behavioral GRIT™ framework and covers key takeaways in leading an organization that implements behavioral science. Behavioral GRIT™ stands for the business functions related to Goals, Research, Innovation, and Testing.

The chapters are complemented by an appendix which covers ideas to introduce behavioral science initiatives. I argue that first a company needs to identify its goals and identify what type of predominant organization model it wants to pursue. There are five predominant organizational models I've seen. I also offer that a company should consider a number of implementation elements that may play a role during execution. Example elements include an advisory board and a behavioral science officer.

Note that the purpose of this book is not to teach people about behavioral science; there are many other books out there for those purposes. That said, *Inside Nudging* introduces some behavioral science concepts to provide context and help develop a common language between management professionals and scientists.

I see the application of behavioral science as still being in the early adoption phase. Many companies will benefit if they take time to develop the right approach. I hope *Inside Nudging* helps you with your journey.

Stephen Shu
July 2016

Updates for the release of *Nudging Democratized*:

Since the original release of *Inside Nudging*, I have decided to continue the discourse on implementing behavioral science by adding Chapter 7 entitled, "Nudging to Democratize Outcomes". Like Chapter 5 which touches on nudging and ethics, the material in Chapter 7 is important to me in terms of my values and implementing behavioral science for good.

Stephen Shu
July 2019

1
BEHAVIORAL SCIENCE CENTERED DESIGN IS THE NEW BLACK

People love to debate design, whether they have even thought about what design really means or what it should mean. Design permeates the senses, micro interactions between things and people, and culture. But how does one define design?

Rather than trying to define design, let's first contemplate design by taking a look at what some others think about the recently launched, much-awaited Apple Watch. For example, in an article in Fortune magazine (Leaf 2015), a number of accomplished designers shared their thoughts about misunderstandings about design and the Apple Watch. Comments included:

- "[The biggest misconception is] that it's about making things pretty."
- "The mistaken belief that we need design for everything."
- "The mistake is attributing to design a cerebral quality that is not necessarily there…"
- "…Apple missed an opportunity to redefine why the tiny screen is on our wrist at all."
- "…I don't think [the Apple Watch] simplifies my life."

- "[The Apple Watch] was a good try. Let's see what comes next."

What about people I know? When I asked my teenage son what he thought about the Apple Watch, although he does not have one (but plays with it extensively every time we go to the Apple Store), he thought it was a big success; it was very cool. Another behavioral scientist I work with quite closely (and a design aficionado I might add) surprised me by telling me he loves his Apple Watch; it makes the weather conditions easily accessible and provides simplified alerts regarding upcoming meetings so that his phone doesn't need to be out. Personally, I would find it hard to displace my current watch, an heirloom from my father that I treasure and keep with me at all times.

Based on these very limited accounts, the definition of design seems to reside in the eye of the beholder. Design often aspires to more than visual beauty. Design can provide utility, support emotional needs, and redefine relationships.

Let's zoom in on the topic of design and utility for a moment by thinking about a coffeepot. What are some purposes of a coffeepot? Well for one thing, some people like coffeepots to hold multiple servings of coffee, say four to ten servings. Coffeepots might be designed to minimize heat escaping, thus keeping the coffee warm. And some people like coffeepots to look nice, say if the coffeepot is used to serve guests.

Now consider Carelman's Coffepot for Masochists (ImpossibleObjects.com n.d.), the core concept of which is also referenced in the book, *Design of Everyday Things* (Norman 2014). The coffeepot looks like it can satisfy most of the purposes mentioned above. Can you get coffee out of it though without burning your hands? How much do you love your coffee?

Although one can probably get coffee out of the coffeepot, and one might even be able to get coffee out without burning their hands, the design makes it hard to use. The design gets in the way of a typical, primary function for a coffeepot. The design burns most people.

How much do you love your coffee?

References: Drawing adapted from Carelman's Coffeepot for Masochists as developed and distributed by ImpossibleObjects.com

Copyright © 2019 by Steve Shu Consulting

Figure 1.1: Carelman's Coffeepot

So is Carelman's Coffeepot for Masochists wrong? I find the design both hilarious and ingenious. A lot of thought went into the design, with obvious purposes to make it both funny and extremely memorable.

Accidental Versus Deliberate Behavioral Architecture

Let's change gears to consider another design example, loosely based on an employer that I was working with and related to processes for getting their employees to save for retirement. Employer processes for getting employees to save vary substantially. For example, some employers may automatically enroll employees into retirement plans and assign them a default savings rate (often as a percentage of pay) and investment mix unless the employee actively decides to opt out or change their elections. Other employers may make blank forms available so that employees can enroll if they both choose to do so and make positive selections. Yet other employers make retirement savings enrollment an opt-in process, yet quick and easy.

The employer I was working with chose to use a flavor of this latter approach. I say flavor because I'll make a case that that while the spirit and intentions of the approach are good, the detailed design has issues. Take a look at the next figure to get a flavor of their approach.

Should we design choice processes certain ways just because we can?

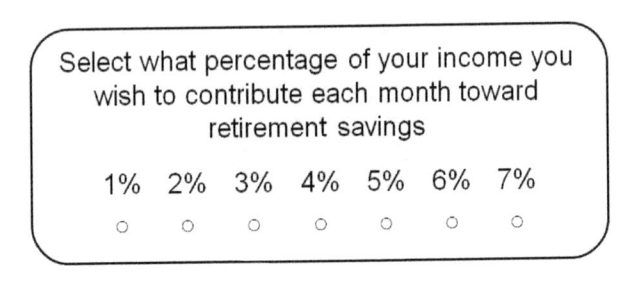

> Select what percentage of your income you wish to contribute each month toward retirement savings
>
> 1% 2% 3% 4% 5% 6% 7%
> ○   ○   ○   ○   ○   ○   ○

Source: Adapted based on field experience

Copyright © 2019 by Steve Shu Consulting

Figure 1.2: Illustration of Accidental Architecture

I think the employer created this form mostly because they could; they didn't think deeply enough about what they were trying to achieve and connect those goals with behavioral science and design. They wanted to make selections easy, so they implemented a fill-in-the-bubble approach to having employees select the desired percentage of income to contribute to retirement savings.

Let's look more closely at this design relative to goals. Now without going into a lot of details (we'll cover a related example in Chapter 2), one can make a pretty strong case that in the United States, employees on average should be saving at least ten percent of their pay toward retirement (Benartzi and Lewin 2012). If the employer wants to support the goal of getting employees to save at least ten percent (which they did want), then how does this design support that goal? For example, if a person wants to save ten percent or more, the design doesn't even support this type of entry by the user.

Now let's also briefly examine this design relative to behavioral science research. On the one hand, studies have shown that primacy influences choice, e.g., items first on a list tend to get chosen more often (Mantonakis, et al. 2009). So this raises a question whether people will tend to select 1% as their option more often than they should, especially since we tend to read from left to right in the US. Additionally, studies in other areas suggest circumstances where biases such as edge aversion (e.g., aversion to the choices at the extreme ends) and middle bias (e.g., focusing on the choice in the center) (Attali and Bar-Hillel Summer 2003) might play a role. Perhaps 4% percent might end up being a bias point. Finally, should the design even have seven choices at all? Setting the proper contribution rate might seem more complicated to employees than it should be, and the employer may find the people failing to sign up due to complexity and choice overload issues (Iyengar 2011).

So while the employer wants to implement an easy design and have their employees achieve good outcomes (i.e., secure retirements), hasty design can lead to accidental design, which in turn, can get in the way and burn users like Carelman's Coffeepot.

To get out of the accidental design business, we need to think deliberately about design architecture, and preferably behavioral architecture. Choice architecture was a term coined by Richard Thaler and Cass Sunstein in their book, *Nudge: Improving Decisions About Health, Wealth, and Happiness* (Thaler and Sunstein 2008). In the introduction to their book, they relate the case of administrators in a city school system reconsidering how to arrange the food in the cafeterias where kids eat. To help illustrate this, look at the following figure and put yourself in the administrators' shoes. Assuming you couldn't change the menu itself, where would you physically place the desserts? How should you decide where the healthy food should go?

Consider how we should place food in the serving area.

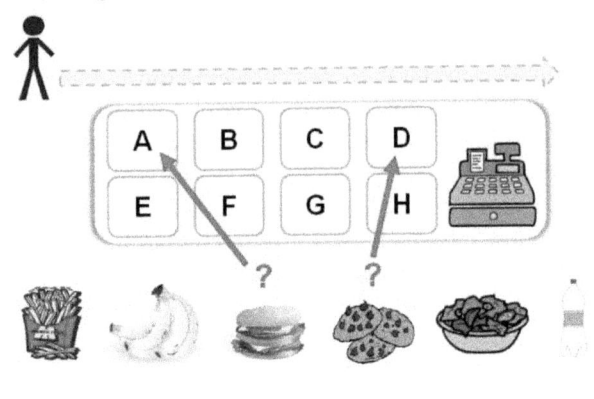

Figure 1.3: Illustration of Choice Architecture

In the case related by Thaler and Sunstein, administrators realized that the demand for items could be increased or decreased by as much as 25 percent depending on where the food was placed.

The administrators act as choice architects; they have the power to influence food selected based on setting the structure of the environment. And because food has to be placed somewhere, there is no neutral design. That is, all designs influence choice somehow; they nudge people in some direction. Some designs will increase the selection of the cookies. Others will increase the selection of bananas.

Which then begs questions as to both the goals of the architects and the design strategies that should be used. Should the goal be to maximize profits based on the markup on each item? Should the strategy be to place food randomly? Should the goal be to make students better off? We'll revisit the concept of goals throughout the cases in this book. Later on we'll also focus on ethical considerations and people's perceptions.

Architects have power over not only choices, but also information and process. Consider the following screenshot, which is from a *Wired* article covering Merrill Lynch's implementation of a website that takes a photo of a user. This photo is then put in a virtual time machine so that user can see what they will look like in the future (Wohlsen 2012). The tool is loosely based on research by Hal Hershfield at UCLA and colleagues (Hershfield, et al. 2011).

Without evaluating the merits of this design, Merrill Lynch's implementation has some very interesting and notable aspects. In the center of the screen there is the age progressed photo of the user, which provides information as to what they might look like in retirement. As another example of information presented to the user, the right hand panel illustrates what a gallon of gasoline is projected to cost decades into the future (in the year 2082 it is apparently expected to be $39.88 per gallon). The user can also see how the cost of living will be up 939% from what it is today.

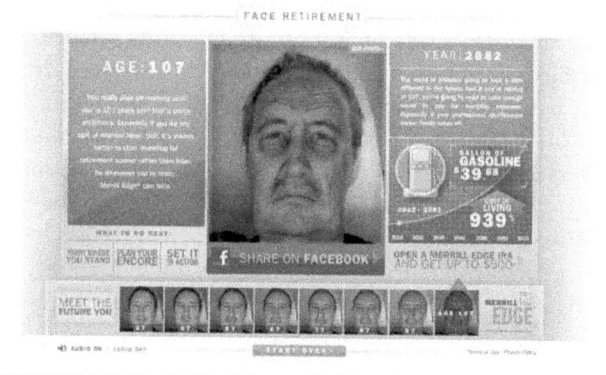

Figure 1.4: Illustration of Other Behavioral Architecture Considerations

But one could also imagine a different approach to information architecture. What if gasoline was stated in today's real dollars versus nominal dollars in the future? Or what if dollars were stated in annual costs instead of dollars per gallon? Yet why even use gasoline as an example of the future? What if healthcare costs were put on the screen? The designer has control over what information is displayed and how information is displayed.

Also notice the button just below the center photo which reads, "Share on Facebook." That might be the best process approach if the goal is to create marketing buzz and allow the user to connect with others. One could also imagine other designs though, such as a process of enabling a user to increase their retirement savings if they feel emotionally connected to their future self. In the original study by Hershfield and colleagues involving retirement savings, participants who saw age-progressed photos increased savings by 30% (average savings rate of 6.76%) relative to a alternative group (average savings rate of 5.20%), who instead saw photos of their current self (Hershfield, et al. 2011). So in addition to information architecture, process architecture is another important consideration in design.[4]

Power, Tools, and Devil in the Details

Nudging, which I'll loosely define here as the consideration of architecture and application of behavioral science, started to establish a beachhead in the public policy space after Thaler and Sunstein's released *Nudge* in 2008. A couple of years later in 2010, the Behavioral Insights Team (or Nudge Unit) emerged in the UK (Behavioral Insights Team Annual update 2010-11 2011). In 2014, the White House set up the Social and Behavioral Sciences Team. By their first birthday in February 2015, they had success with various pilot projects, covering areas like connecting veterans with counseling, helping student borrowers better understand loan repayment possibilities, and re-enrolling Armed Services members in savings plans (Shankar 2015). Nudging initiatives in the public policy space are also present in some countries within the European Union, Canada, Singapore, and New Zealand (Ly and Soman 2013).

---

[4] At this point, I do not plan to delve into the intricacies of the definitions for information, choice, and process architecture since the scope of these terms can get muddied just like architecture terms related to buildings, such as modern, classical, or contemporary architecture. That said, I will revisit process architecture in greater detail in Chapter 4.

While nudging activity in the public policy space is still formative and crossing the chasm[5], we are now seeing more activity outside of public policy. Some examples of companies and organizations harnessing the power of behavioral science to achieve great results include:

- **GymPact** – This startup uses a choice architecture construct of pre-commitment to get people to exercise or pay, yielding 80 to 90 percent follow-through in exercise (Kim 2012).
- **Opower** – This software company leverages information architecture constructs with personalized energy reports; solutions have helped residents save $355 million in energy in less than five years (Cialdini 2013).
- **HM Revenue and Customs (HMRC) and Behavioral Insights Team (BIT)** – By using information architecture and highlighting social norms, they increased clearance of delinquent tax payments from 67.5% to 83% (Behavioral Insights Team Annual update 2010-11 2011).

It is important to re-emphasize that the application of behavioral science requires attention to details, and even a simple taxonomy of approaches relative to the design of defaults[6] in choice architecture reveals that the design considerations can be significant. See the following figure for a

---

[5] Based on the countries listed in the prior sources and accounting method used, very roughly 3% to 10% of countries in the world have nudging efforts in the public policy space.
[6] For readers unfamiliar with the use of the term "defaults" in this context, these are essentially pre-selected choices made for an individual unless they opt-out of the choice entirely (if possible) or actively select another choice option. An often-used example is the notion of organ donation in the case of death where in some countries the default when applying for a driver's license is *not* to donate organs upon death versus other countries the default is to donate organs upon death. In the case of organ donation, a simple difference in choice architecture can have a dramatic impact on saving lives (Johnson and Goldstein 2003).

sample (Goldstein, et al. 2008). Since I don't want to re-invent the wheel, I leave the reader to investigate the sources I've listed and many others I've not listed. That said, this is a good time to point out the noteworthy concept of personalized defaults, where choice architecture is determined according to the characteristics of the individual making the choice. As the world evolves in the digital space with videos, social graphs, big data, mobile technology, the Internet of things (IoT), and the like, there are tremendous research and innovation opportunities with behavioral science and personalization. These opportunities will just continue to increase over time.

Just within choice realm, you have many design choices for defaults.

Mass Defaults
- Lowest cost / lowest risk defaults
- Random defaults
- Forced or active choices
- Benign defaults
- Hidden option

Personalized Defaults
- Persistent defaults
- Smart defaults
- Adaptive defaults

Source: Goldstein, D. et al. "Nudge Your Customers Toward Better Choices." *Harvard Business Review* (2008)

Copyright © 2019 by Steve Shu Consulting

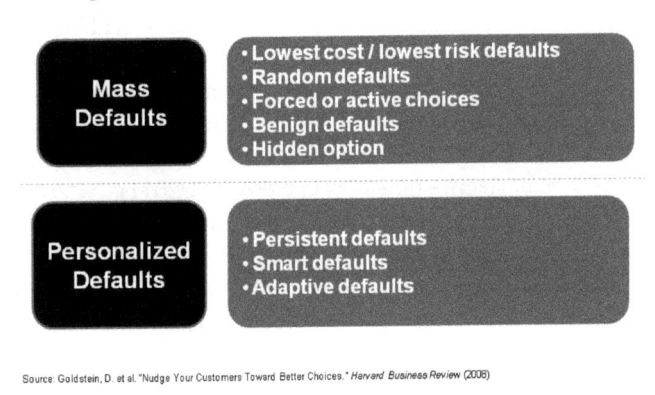

Figure 1.5: Summary of Potential Design Choices for Defaults

Behavioral GRIT™

To me the term "grit" means having the ability and fortitude to succeed. Based on my experience and gleaning from that of others, I wanted to put together an investigative framework that would help companies assess, plan, and take action to apply behavioral science. I call this framework Behavioral GRIT™. GRIT stands for the business functions related to Goals, Research, Innovation, and Testing. In my experience, the best companies make deliberate choices to design and improve these functions when examining them through a behavioral science lens (which includes considering information, choice, and process architecture with a varying degree of personalization).

Structurally, I see this framework targeted toward companies that wish to innovate and create something new of value, whether it be a new way of thinking that results in better outcomes or new products and services. That said, there are clearly other possibilities to use the framework on a more incremental basis (e.g., to see if there are areas that can be tuned up by incorporating behavioral science).

Does your organization have the Behavioral GRIT™ to win?

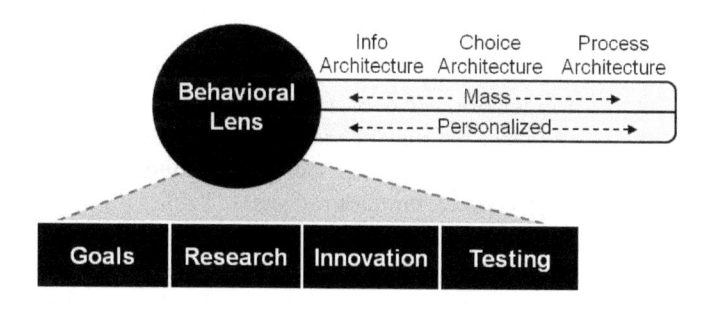

Figure 1.6: Behavioral GRIT™ Overview

The Behavioral GRIT™ framework may seem intuitive, even obvious, but failure to determine goals and understand previous research before jumping into innovation and testing can easily lead organizations astray. There have been cases where behavioral science academics, who know the research well, jump into an organization and start recommending solutions before understanding the problems the organization faces (goals). There have also been situations where organizations start trying to design interventions without understanding what has already been tested in the past (research). Walking through each step in the Behavioral GRIT™ framework ensures that the ultimate recommendations are both optimized to the goal and well grounded in previous work.

In subsequent chapters, I'll go into more detail about the consideration areas and illustrate Behavioral GRIT™ using cases of companies that apply behavioral science.

Key Takeaways
1. **Plan to incubate the use of behavioral science lenses** - Think about design through behavioral science lenses of information, choice, and process architecture. Additionally, consider mass versus personalized approaches. If organizational knowledge needs to be expanded, consider incremental investment in education for the organization, contracting out, or partnering. Also consider the notion of behavioral assessment frameworks or components that may be available as lenses for specific areas (e.g., website analysis).
2. **Map out how your design connects to goals and ethical considerations** – While I'll address this topic in greater detail through cases and the perspectives of and papers by academics, try to make sure that you think about the design architecture elements and ask questions like, "How do these support the goals of our organization, customers, or partners?" and "How does the design support the ethical considerations?"
3. **Start to think about the business processes you'll use to increase organizational IQ around tools and academic literature** – Be aware that behavioral science covers a lot of space and that tools and literature go both broad and deep. Laundry lists of principles can sometimes play a role when thinking about behavioral science, and I'll address under what conditions this may make more or less sense because sometimes it does not. When thinking about tools and literature, at minimum acknowledge and distinguish general (e.g., psychology), industry-specific (e.g., finance), and sub-industry-specific research (e.g., finance and annuities versus Social Security).

4. **Recognize that behavioral science research can have deep, shallow, repeatable, charted, uncharted, and mysterious territory simultaneously** – While behavioral science can explain a lot, it cannot explain many aspects of human behavior, even when looking at broad swathes of people. Puzzles exist. Additionally, even when broad explanations exist as borne out in peer reviewed research, we should acknowledge variances between individuals. Finally, even when research exists and has been broadly replicated, there may be differences observed when these are taken to the field or actual implementations.

2
ORGANIZATIONS CAN PACKAGE BEHAVIORAL SCIENCE FOR GOOD

In the fall of 2010, I was driving to the Luxe Sunset Boulevard Hotel in Los Angeles for a meeting over drinks. Honestly, I can't remember exactly how this meeting got set up. I do know my wife deserves tremendous credit for more reasons that I can mention. At the Chicago business school where she got her PhD[7], she got involved with behavioral economics circa-1997 before it got really hot circa-2008 in the public sector with the book *Nudge* (Thaler and Sunstein 2008). Given *Nudge*'s success in 2008-09, the stars were starting to align by 2010 with a limited number of private sector companies looking to do something very unique. Although I didn't know it yet, my wife was introducing me to one of those special companies, Allianz Global Investors. My wife probably mentioned my background in helping companies with start-up initiatives within larger companies. So my meeting was going to be with two people, Shlomo Benartzi and Cathy Smith, to

---

[7] My wife is now a marketing professor at the UCLA Anderson School of Management. She was trained in behavioral economics at Chicago Booth, and her PhD advisors were Richard Thaler, France LeClerc, Yuval Rottenstreich, and George Wu.

discuss possibilities of me helping out with an initiative they had just started with support from top management at Allianz Global Investors. Little did I know this meeting would mark the beginning of an experience that would turn out to be one of the most fulfilling professional experiences of my career.

The Allianz Global Investors Center for Behavioral Finance (the Center) was founded in 2010 with the goal to turn academic insights into actionable ideas and practical tools (Allianz Global Investors n.d.). Shlomo Benartzi, a prominent academic at the UCLA Anderson School of Management in behavioral finance, was serving as Chief Behavioral Economist and provided the scientific vision and guidance for the Center. Cathy Smith, a Director at Allianz Global Investors, served as Co-Director for the Center and provided business leadership for the Center at both strategy and operational levels. The role I played at the Center would evolve over the years, given my modus operandi as a long-time management consultant. That said, a key role for me involved bridging academic insights into implementation, such as facilitating innovation, tools, content, and initiative development.

The first program the Center rolled out was called PlanSuccess™[8], and it fell into the general category of efforts to help people save enough money so that they could eventually retire with dignity. Although I am biased, the program blossomed to become an extremely fine example of combining thought leadership, science, and practical application through a diverse ecosystem of academics, employees, and partners (see Figure 2.1). According to an article by Fred Barstein published around the Center's fifth birthday, the Center had "rocked the [defined contribution] world" and was one of only two investment-only firms to receive special recognition for its value-add program (Barstein 2015).

---

[8] PlanSuccess is a registered US trademark of Allianz Global Investors Capital LLC as of October 6, 2015.

The initiative involves diverse people working together.

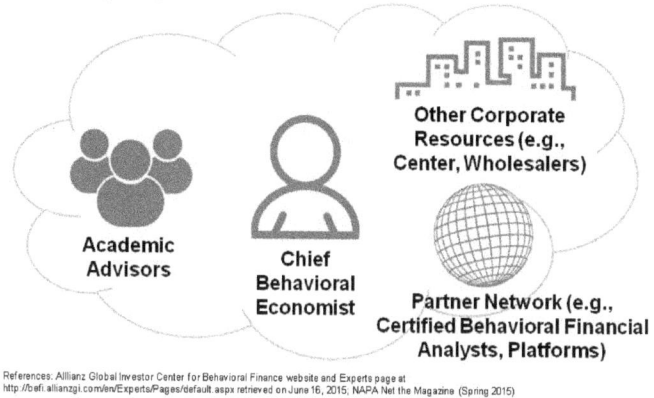

- Academic Advisors
- Chief Behavioral Economist
- Other Corporate Resources (e.g., Center, Wholesalers)
- Partner Network (e.g., Certified Behavioral Financial Analysts, Platforms)

References: Allianz Global Investor Center for Behavioral Finance website and Experts page at http://befi.allianzgi.com/en/Experts/Pages/default.aspx retrieved on June 16, 2015; NAPA Net the Magazine (Spring 2015)
Copyright © 2019 by Steve Shu Consulting

Figure 2.1: The PlanSuccess Ecosystem

An Executive-Level Look at the PlanSuccess Case Study

First, let's take a look at one of the core problems within the retirement space in the United States, which is also happening to differing degrees in the other areas of the world. In the United States on an aggregate level, employers have moved from a defined benefit (DB) world to a defined contribution (DC) world. This shift has generally been initiated by employers over the years to reduce their costs and their liabilities from increasing life expectancies. In the DB world, employees essentially accumulate future retirement income by simply going to work. In a DC world, employees must decide to participate in the retirement plan (often a 401k plan), decide how much to save, and decide what investments to put their money into. Suffice it to say, the shift in the tide from DB to DC has created both opportunities and challenges. Out of every ten people in the United States, five can save through a 401k plan, three actually save, and one saves enough (though one can debate how wisely) (Benartzi and Lewin 2012). See Figure 2.2 for a summary of the retirement crisis.

Let's look at a key problem statement in the DC space.

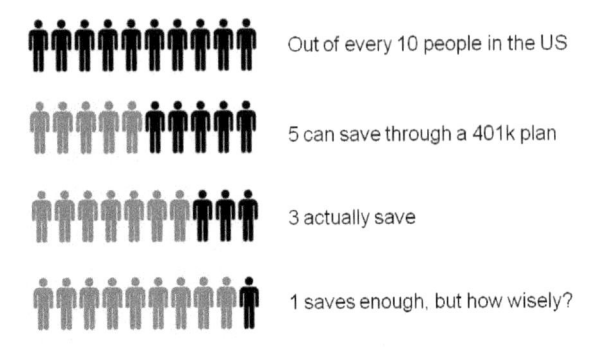

👥👥👥👥👥 Out of every 10 people in the US

👥👥👥👥👥 5 can save through a 401k plan

👥👥👥👥👥 3 actually save

👥👥👥👥👥 1 saves enough, but how wisely?

Source: Adapted from Benartzi and Lewin, Save More Tomorrow: Practical Behavioral Finance Solutions to Improve 401k Plans (2012)
Copyright © 2019 by Steve Shu Consulting

Figure 2.2: A Perspective on the Retirement Crisis

For the PlanSuccess program, the focus of the effort was on a subset of the larger problem of retirement savings. Namely, how can individuals that have access to a 401k plan be helped? A first step was to articulate where individuals run into issues (e.g., as evidenced by poor outcomes or behaviorally unhealthy plan designs) and then offering design solutions. A key strength of the PlanSuccess approach was the creation of a framework that connected behavioral science with the business problem and desired outcomes. See Figure 2.3, which comes from the Center's website (Allianz Global Investors Center for Behavioral Finance n.d.). The columns reflect the behavioral science challenges (e.g., Inertia, Loss Aversion, Myopia) that people face, the rows reflect the business problem of getting people to Save, Save More, and Save Smarter[9], and the cells

---

[9] The notion of 90-10-90 outcomes was a key point of view put forth in the book, *Save More Tomorrow*, and represents a rule-of-thumb notion that a good goal is to get at least 90 percent of people participating in a defined contribution plan (i.e., SAVE), have participants saving at least 10 percent of salary presuming a generous employer match (i.e., SAVE MORE), and have at least 90 percent investing wisely (i.e., SAVE SMARTER)

within the matrix represent the proposed behavioral finance solutions (e.g., Match Optimizer, Save More Tomorrow 1.0) to help employers design behaviorally-healthy retirements plans for their employees.

The Center facilitated and created a number of actionable ideas and tools to support the PlanSuccess program, including the *Save More Tomorrow* book (Benartzi and Lewin 2012), an online PlanSuccess Behavioral Audit tool (Allianz Global Investors n.d.), a Certified Behavioral Finance Analyst program, and other content (Allianz Global Investors n.d.).

The PlanSuccess method is notable as it provides a product-agnostic approach to improving DC plans and outcomes for future retirees. Allianz Global Investors developed the PlanSuccess Behavioral Audit tool for use by network partners (e.g., Certified Behavioral Finance Analysts). Network partners use the tool to perform behavioral audits of employer DC plans and make recommendations to the employer based on behavioral science. To give a flavor of PlanSuccess behavioral audit questions, here are a few (Benartzi and Lewin 2012):

- Does your plan use auto-enrollment for new employees? (This question examines inertia.)
- What is the maximum percentage of pay that the employer will match? (This question addresses loss aversion for the employer and examines anchoring for the participant.)
- Do account statements show participants their projected income at retirement given their current savings trajectory? (This question examines myopia.)

(Benartzi and Lewin 2012).

3x3 framework connects behavioral science with the business problem.

	EASY CHOICES (*Inertia*)	MANAGED LOSSES (Loss Aversion)	BEHAVIORAL TIME MACHINES (*Myopia*)
SAVE	Auto-Takeoff	Match Optimizer	The Face Tool
SAVE MORE	Save More Tomorrow 1.0	Save More Tomorrow 2.0	Imagine Exercise
SAVE SMARTER	Investment Solutions Pyramid	Lifetime Statement	Tangible Account Statement

Reference: Allianz Global Investors Center for Behavioral Finance website, http://befi.allianzgi.com/en/save-more-tomorrow/Pages/key-themes-of-the-book.aspx retrieved June 15, 2015
Copyright © 2019 by Steve Shu Consulting

Figure 2.3: Cornerstone Framework to PlanSuccess ("The 3x3 Matrix")

Looking a bit deeper at the behavioral audit, a premise of behavioral science is that the details matter. So if one zooms in on the intersection of the SAVE row and Inertia column relative to 401k plan design, there are specific behavioral audit checkpoints with respect to the choice architecture being implemented by the employer. Behavioral audit checkpoints include:

- Use of auto-enrollment (opt-out defaults) for new employees
- Use of auto-enrollment (opt-out defaults) for existing employees
- Initial default saving rate
- Use of active (prompted) choice
- Use of easy choice
- Use of future (pre-commitment) enrollment

Now if you recall the Behavioral GRIT™ framework I mentioned in Chapter 1, I made not only a distinction between choice, information, and process architecture, but also a distinction between the use of mass and personalized approaches. In theory, one could imagine taking the

PlanSuccess framework further by going deeper into any of these dimensions. For example, the existing 401k plan design world largely involves mass architecture approaches. One could imagine a new 401k world with more personalization (e.g., tailored nudges for individuals) given advances in technology. A digital world enables new possibilities.

Yet while there are new possibilities, it is worthwhile to note that the PlanSuccess 3x3 framework leverages significant, specialized research. It is neither always possible nor desirable to try to bypass this part of the process (I'll address the topic of research and nuances of applying research in business settings in Chapter 6). For example, the Save More Tomorrow research (Thaler and Benartzi 2004) involved significant innovation and controlled testing that began back in 1998. See Figure 2.4 (Allianz n.d.) for an illustration related to the Save More Tomorrow research and how results were measured over time for three distinct groups of people (i.e., those that declined consultation, those that made a one-off savings increase, and those that elected Save More Tomorrow for regular, automatic savings increases).

3x3 framework uses significant, specialized research...here's an example.

Deferral Rates Increased from 3.5% to 13.6% in Four Years Using Save More Tomorrow

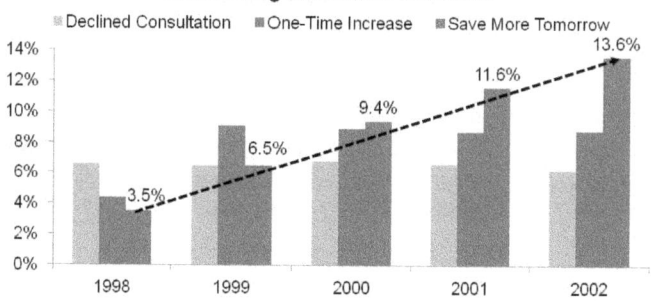

Year	Declined Consultation	One-Time Increase	Save More Tomorrow
1998		3.5%	
1999		6.5%	
2000			9.4%
2001			11.6%
2002			13.6%

Reference: Thaler and Benartzi (2004) with graphic retrieved from http://knowledge.allianz.com/finance/behavioral_finance/?1818/save-more-tomorrow-pension-savings-rates#popup-information-1994 on July 8, 2015
Copyright © 2019 by Steve Shu Consulting

Figure 2.4: An Example of Specialized Research – Save More Tomorrow

Let's recap. Allianz Global Investors created a Center for

Behavioral Finance, which provided thought leadership and was essentially an innovation center[10]. The Center was dedicated to creating tools and content and reinvented the notion of services that could be provided by the industry and its ecosystem partners. The 3x3 framework was published as part of the book, *Save More Tomorrow*, and any advisor or plan sponsor could start to use the behavioral finance principals contained within that book to help design behaviorally-healthy DC plans. Allianz went further by creating the PlanSuccess Behavioral Audit tool and a support network for an elite set of financial advisors that earned the Certified Behavioral Financial Analyst designation through a specialized training program.

What kind of impact could PlanSuccess have on a company and its employees? FiduciaryFirst was one of the early retirement advisory firms that provided significant input during the creation of PlanSuccess. Figure 2.5 provides a nice summary of the amazing results that FiduciaryFirst and a client company achieved by using PlanSuccess (FiduciaryFirst n.d.). Participation in the DC plan offered by the company increased from 45% to 87% of employees actively saving in the retirement plan as a percentage of total eligible employees. Deferral rates (i.e., average percent of income saved by each employee) increased from 2.9% to 7.2%. And the percentage of participants saving smarter (defined as investing in a diversified, one-stop solution) increased from 24% to 79%. Those results indicate that significantly more people should have significantly more money at retirement than they would have otherwise. Jamie Hayes, Partner at FiduciaryFirst, said[11], "It has been great to work with the Allianz Global Investors Center for Behavioral Finance, employers, record keepers, and other advisors over the years. I worked with Shlomo Benartzi, Cathy Smith, and Steve Shu on the Save More Tomorrow book, PlanSuccess tool, and Certified Behavioral Financial Analyst training program from the very beginning when they

---

[10] In Appendix A, I discuss the notion of innovation centers as well as other predominant organizational models and implementation elements for implementing behavioral science initiatives.

[11] Personal correspondence with Jamie Hayes (October 2015)

were just ideas and pencil and paper tools. Now we've developed a sense of scale and impact. And we've done a large part in changing the industry. We've helped employers remove behavioral obstacles in their DC plans, and those efforts directly translate into improving the lives of future retirees. I'm extremely proud of that legacy."

Advisors can implement behavioral finance to help their clients' employees retire with dignity.

	SAVE 93% Increase	SAVE MORE 148% Increase	SAVE SMARTER 229% Increase
Before	45%	2.9%	24%
After	87%	7.2%	79%
	Participation Rate	Deferral Rate	Participants in a Diversified One Stop Portfolio Solution

Source: http://fiduciaryfirst.com/participant-effect retrieved July 20, 2016 and updated based on correspondence with Jamie Hayes on October 20, 2015.
Copyright © 2019 by Steve Shu Consulting

Figure 2.5: An Example of Successfully Applying Behavioral Finance

Why PlanSuccess Succeeded

In Chapter 1, I introduced the notion of the Behavioral GRIT™ framework, where GRIT stands for the business functions related Goals, Research, Innovation, and Testing. Let's use Behavioral GRIT™ to examine PlanSuccess:

1. **Goals** – The Center found a sweet spot in terms of both aligning goals between various constituents and elevating the whole industry perspective on how to design behaviorally-healthy DC plans.
    - **Company Goals** - The Center was established with the goal of turning academic insights into actionable ideas and practical tools.
    - **Individual and Plan Sponsor Goals** - With the backdrop of the US retirement crisis, goals included helping people to save enough money

so that they could eventually retire with dignity. Helping people make proper decisions would involve helping employers (i.e., plan sponsors) develop behaviorally-healthy DC plans.
- **Industry Goals** – Sometimes thought leadership requires building primary demand (e.g., demand for behaviorally-friendly DC plans across all companies) over selective demand (e.g., demand for specific Allianz Global Investors products and services). The Center focused on primary demand building, making ideas available to all, and being product-agnostic in terms of approach (e.g., there are no mentions of specific products in the book *Save More Tomorrow*).
- **Specific Company Positioning and Network Ecosystem Goals** - Goals included maintaining an elite position in the market and fostering a high-touch partner experience. As a consequence, a premium network and program for Certified Behavioral Financial Analysts was created. An online version of the PlanSuccess tool could be used by certified professionals, who essentially distribute the knowledge of behavioral finance by applying the concepts to employer DC plans.

2. **Research** – The Center created a scientific leadership position along with an advisory board to harness scientific knowledge that was mostly developed outside of Allianz Global Investors and within the academic community.
    - **Behavioral Science Officer** – To spearhead scientific vision, the Center created a Chief Behavioral Economist position.
    - **Advisory Board** - Specialized experts outside of Allianz Global Investors and from broader areas like psychology, behavioral economics, finance, and marketing were appointed to an academic advisory board. These experts

provided a combination of input on the broad direction of programs and specific, detailed consultation on design of program elements (e.g., tool development).

- **Specialists and Research Consultants** – In order to support tool creation, data analysis, content development (e.g., whitepapers, presentations), talks, and some field research, the Center utilized a small set of scientifically-skilled resources to execute its programs.
- **Specialized Research** – If one looks at the research called out in the book *Save More Tomorrow*, the 3x3 framework leveraged decades of pre-existing, industry- and sub-industry-specific literature. This minimized the need for new research and benefited the PlanSuccess efforts in terms of time-to-market.

3. **Innovation** – Arguably, innovation is one of the trickiest areas to get right. Volumes of books could be written on the subject. In Chapter 4, I will address a few key angles I see as especially important for behavioral science applications. For the case of PlanSucesss, the Center basically put together the right team and had a maniacal focus on design.
    - **Diverse Team** – I mentioned the advisory board previously, and the Center went further to collaborate with partners and clients to make sure that designs went beyond the lab and could be used in the real world.
    - **Unique Resources** – There are some aspects of the innovation process that are quite difficult to scale. A trick is synthesizing deep academic insights, deep industry knowledge, design, and development capabilities. It is rare to find individual people that have two of these four capabilities, yet the Center tapped into a very limited number of individuals who each probably have three or four of these capabilities.
    - **Design Focus** – As emphasized in Chapter 1,

design is key. There are a couple of mantras in behavioral economics that "small changes can make a big difference" and that "details matter." But there is another aspect to what the Center did with PlanSuccess from a design-level in terms of changing the meaning and relationship between Certified Behavioral Financial Analysts and plan sponsors. No longer did discussions need to be constrained to the typical story of the 3Fs (i.e., funds, fees, and fiduciary responsibilities). Now the context of the discussion could be changed and extended to the design of behaviorally-healthy DC plans that would help real people.

4. **Testing** – Of the Behavioral GRIT™ areas, testing might be the most straightforward area from a conceptual perspective. Although there are many flavors of testing, two keys for the Center were finding the right partners and testing the tools in the field.

- **Network Collaborators** – As I mentioned earlier, during the creation of PlanSuccess, the Center got input from financial advisory firms, like FiduciaryFirst. The Center also got input from other parties in the DC ecosystem, like recordkeeping firms, consultants, and policy advisors.
- **Field Testing** – Not only did the Center get feedback from intermediate partners like the financial advisors, but the Center also got input from actual plan sponsors that were open to having their DC plans examined from a behavioral health perspective.

Key Takeaways

1. **As you begin to think about implementing new initiatives, think about Behavioral GRIT™** - This includes exploring the goals of constituents, your plans for incorporating research (more in Chapter 6), the context and processes regarding innovation (more in Chapter 4), and capabilities

and processes for testing (more in Chapter 6). In this chapter, we saw that the stars were very aligned for the PlanSuccess efforts, although I hinted that some aspects might be more difficult to replicate to other situations, such as leveraging an existing base of specialized research and acquiring unique resources for innovation.

2. **Don't forget to consider other subareas of behavioral architecture and the degree of personalization** – As I alluded to in this chapter, the 3x3 framework for PlanSucess mostly addresses information and choice architecture considerations. The notion of process architecture (which will be discussed in Chapter 4) is largely unaddressed. And the DC world as a whole is largely built around mass approaches (e.g., as opposed to personalized approaches). So that is also an area of the world that is largely unaddressed. Whether addressing these areas is appropriate or achievable is another story, but you should at least consider unaddressed areas (see Figure 1.6 in Chapter 1).

3. **Remember to think about the organizational model and key implementation elements you'll need to succeed** – Here Allianz Global Investors utilized an Innovation Center model at its core, along with an Advisory Board. I call these the predominant organizational model and implementation elements. To implement a behavioral science initiative, a company generally uses one predominant organizational model. I outline five predominant organizational models in Appendix A. A company can then use multiple implementation elements, such as an advisory board, a behavioral audit, or education program. I also outlined a number of implementation elements in Appendix A.

3
LEARN FROM PROJECT-BASED APPROACHES AND LEVERAGE CONSULTING ORGANIZATIONS

Consulting can be a difficult profession to understand for a number of reasons. On the one hand, getting an opportunity to peek at consulting deliverables is scarce, and as such, most people have no idea what a deliverable might look like. And then there's an important part of consulting that you can't see. You can't see the process. You can't see the interviews, the workshops, the working sessions, the executive review meetings, the behind-the-scenes work, or the facilitation of the consulting and client teams. Yet in consulting, the process is an essential part of the deliverable.[12]

But in order to appreciate this chapter, I feel it is important to shed some light on the consultative approach. I'll do this in two parts. First, I'll describe a case that illustrates two important constructs in consulting: 1) the problem statement, and 2) the consulting engagement (i.e., consulting project). After that I'll tell you a story from the consulting trenches.

---

[12] Readers interested an example of a consulting engagement with and without a proper attention to process might be interested in seeing Chapter 11 of my book, *The Consulting Apprenticeship*.

In one consulting engagement that I oversaw, the client wanted to know how much to bid for wireless spectrum, what types of next generation services they could offer with the spectrum, and what the technology architecture might look like. So we basically formed a team of business and technology consultants.

The business consultants looked at things like:
- auction structure and government documents
- competitors and likely strategies
- historical prices for spectrum in other auctions
- sales of blocks of spectrum
- next generation services opportunity potential and financial analysis
- strategy scenario analysis.

The technology consultants looked at things like:
- wireless and wireline architecture options
- technology standards assessment and risk analysis
- services and network capacity analysis
- services and capital expenditure estimation for network buildout and interconnection
- packaged technology services landscape survey.

We put all of the business and technology workstreams together into a consulting engagement for the client. The problem statement is essentially the issue to be solved by the consulting team. The consulting engagement is essentially the project structure for solving the problem statement. If there's one important thing to learn relative to the consulting mindset, it would be the power of project-based thinking.

Now for my story from the trenches, which happened many years ago. The problem statement the client posed to me was to figure out the reasons why they lost tens of millions of dollars in the prior period. The consulting engagement I proposed to them was performing an operational assessment, which involved identifying the major process flows within their sales, operations, and call center organizations. In addition to the process flows, I also assessed aspects of the organization and supporting technology infrastructure. Finally, I applied

Little's Law over and over again (where average inventory equals average throughput times average cycle time) to calibrate the flow of work throughout the organization and to figure out where the failures and bottlenecks were occurring and why. I can't remember exactly when, but at one point I got the sense that they wanted me to find something wrong with one of the senior managers (not present in the meeting) and the way that manager was operating that part of the business. Should I take the hint to augment or adjust the original problem statement?

As I prepared for the closeout of the engagement and delivery of the final report, I was very proud of my analysis and my recommendations. I had been thorough, structured in my approach, fact-driven, and politically astute. As I delivered my recommendations to the executive team, they seemed extremely happy. I had found the sources of their key issues and used a structured approach, which was beyond their expectations. They had a set of facts and a clear blueprint for making adjustments in the organization. Notably though, I didn't find evidence that the senior manager was operating a part of the business improperly. I don't think management was disappointed, but they were somewhat surprised.

Months later I found out that the company was implementing my high priority recommendations, but the executive team went further and terminated employment with the senior manager. My report had not saved the senior manager. I was told something to the effect that the executive team simply got tired of the senior manager complaining and decided to fire him. Even though the termination was not directly related to my work, for some reason I felt scarred. I'm sure the senior manager that was fired felt much worse.

Why did I relate this story? While I have many good stories about consulting, some scars serve as a reminder to me about the nature of consulting. Consulting is centered around problem statements and projects. And when companies look to use consultants, they are often looking for change. The companies that have hired consultants have often pre-committed themselves to changing something. The scar is a reminder to me that consultants may be both change agents and signs of change.

In the following sections, I am going to outline three types of problem statements that may be addressed via leveraging consulting organizations as change agents: Ambitious Problem Statements, Traditional Problem Statements, and Micro-Problem Statements.

The Ambitious Problem Statement and the Skunk Works Project

One extremely successful company that I have worked with had this bold problem statement for the consulting team:

"We don't see our current business operations as sustainable in the long-run. We want to create a new model that eclipses the old one and obsoletes our existing model. We want our new model to continuously incorporate principles from behavioral science."

The company and consulting team approach to that problem statement would include creating a project and devoting an elite, agile team to innovate and disrupt the existing business. A project with such an orientation and approach is essentially a type of Skunk Works®[13].

The Skunks Works story offers instructive lessons for those companies that have ambitious aspirations surrounding innovation. The backdrop in 1943 was that the U.S. Army approached Lockheed Aircraft Corporation with a problem. Due to threats posed by Germany relative to advancing jet technology, the U.S. needed a groundbreaking jet prototype in less than six months (Lockheed Martin Corporation n.d.); the timeframe was extremely short and the prototype needed to travel hundreds of miles per hour faster than Lockheed's current propeller plane (May 2012).

The legendary Kelly Johnson led the elite Lockheed team that was charged with designing and creating the jet. The effort was highly secretive and due to space considerations, the team had to be located in a rented circus tent near a smelly manufacturing plant. Now Li'l Abner was a famous comic strip at the time that sometimes included a smelly place called Skonk Works, a place made foul and toxic smelling by strange brew

---

[13] Skunk Works® is registered trademark of Lockheed Martin Corporation.

concoctions made from ground-up skunks and worn-out shoes. Lockheed team member Irv Culver, a fan of cartoon Li'l Abner, drew a connection to their present working conditions and was often known to answer the phones, saying "Skonk Works, inside man Culver speaking." It was catchy enough that the division later adopted a modified name, Skunk Works. In a miraculous 143 days, the Skunk Works team created from soup-to-nuts the XP-80 jet (Lockheed Martin Corporation n.d.).

Kelly Johnson developed fourteen rules and practices for Skunk Works operations (Lockheed Martin Corporation n.d.). While a number of his principles are specific to military contractors, there are a number of principles that are generalizable to Skunk Works-like projects that other businesses set up. I interpret Kelly's principles and generalize as follows:

- The Skunk Works manager must report to top leadership and have full control of the initiative from research and development all the way to the market and channel.
- The Skunk Works team should be agile, elite, and co-located.
- Team operations should be supported by using simple, flexible design systems (e.g., drawing and release systems), although critical work should be documented thoroughly.
- The team must have the authority to the test the product in initial stages and the final product in live situations.

While the operations that Kelly Johnson led had more restrictions on people within the company that could be connected to the Skunk Works project, from my perspective companies that use Skunk Works-like approaches should feel more free to incorporate learnings back to other areas of the business. Depending on the nature of the business, incorporating learnings might involve regular presentations by the Skunk Works team to the broader company, open houses to kick the tires on prototypes, or learnings being shared on corporate messaging platforms (such as Slack at https://slack.com).

There is one other aspect of the Skunk Works approach that needs to be refined in a modern world. Skunk Works approaches, as the concept spread to other companies, often came into being because those companies had core businesses that were either lagging or losing steam in research and development. Such companies were often mired in bureaucracy or other strategic and operational issues. In a Forbes article, Steve Blank poignantly articulated the need for a new orientation. He advocated, "Skunk works epitomized innovation by exception...Companies now need *innovation by design* – innovation and execution that work side-by-side." (Blank 2014).

It is beyond the scope of this book to cover the breadth of innovation approaches that Skunk Works projects may use. However, I want to point some parts of the innovation approach that are important to think about when implementing behavioral science:

1. **Strategy and Cadence** - Establish clear goals and a strategy for integrating behavioral science from organizational and project cadence perspectives. Innovation is generally a messy process, and some may not be used to being inside such an uncertain, tornado-like environment. Set the right expectations with the team, and establish a cadence and working relationship between behavioral science experts and the rest of the team. It may be desirable to establish a science officer or an advisory board that can effectively interface and work with the product management and development teams. For example, some of the companies I have worked with set regular meetings (e.g., weekly to monthly) with behavioral science experts to develop product strategy, apply behavioral lenses to new prototype designs, and help steer A/B testing[14]. As organizations get more

---

[14] The term A/B testing refers to studies where controlled conditions are measured for differences in outcomes. Using an example from the healthcare space, patients might be randomly assigned to one of two conditions, either A or B, and their

sophisticated, they may add workshops and internal messaging channels to help diffuse behavioral science knowledge more broadly into the organization.
2. **Financial Analysis** - Strengthen organizational capabilities to perform thumbnail financial analysis of the potential impact of behavioral science interventions. When working in innovative environments, teams will inevitably run into many new issues, potential subprojects, and potential solutions. How can the organization prioritize its efforts relative to the volume of opportunities? Having a discipline toward thumbnail financial analysis of each opportunity and approach can help lend another perspective on prioritization. For example, financial analysis might include quantifying what a reduction in customer churn or increase in customer engagement might mean in terms of either annual dollars, lifetime value, or market capitalization impact to the company. And because financial analysis requires attention to details, it can also help the organization gain clarity around behavioral interventions and differentiating between primary- and second-order effects. Sometimes it can be helpful for an organization to assign a point person to perform financial analyses across both large and ad-hoc opportunities.
3. **Cohort Design and Measurement Thinking** - Especially for digital environments, develop ways to measure not only individual micro-level but also cohort behavior. Why is this important? In behavioral economics, while there is the mantra that details matter and that every part of a design

---

recovery time measured as an outcome variable. In Condition A patients might be given a placebo pill while in Condition B patients might be given a pill that contains actual active ingredients. The data can be statistically analyzed to see to what extent there are differences in recovery time outcomes for patients assigned to either of the two conditions.

needs to be scrutinized (e.g., in terms of visual layout, information and choice architecture), in Skunk Works projects one might be rethinking everything from the individual parts to the whole design. Yes, details matter, *but so does the big picture* (the latter is not always addressed in behavioral economics literature I've seen). That's where cohort design and measurement thinking come in. Cohort measurements involve taking a step back and looking at behavior at a higher level (such as in terms of customer engagement and how many different ways a customer has interacted with the company) versus a lower level (such as the number of customer web pageviews). Ideally this is done for groups of similar people as viewed by the company. See Figure 3.1 which illustrates the notion of cohort measurements and is motivated by content in Eric Ries' book, *The Lean Startup* (Ries 2011).

Use cohorts to measure high-level behavior.

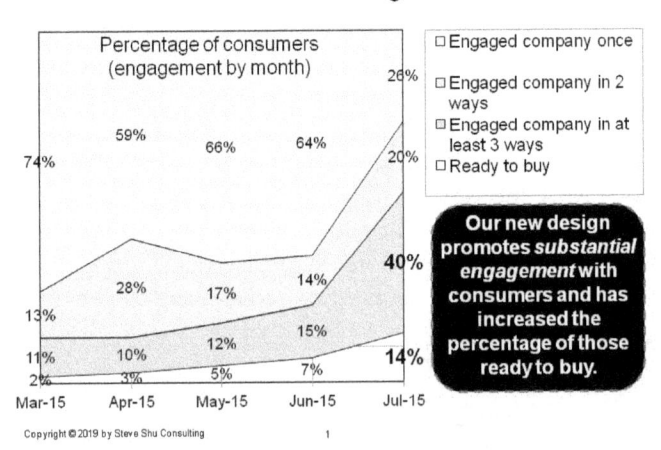

Percentage of consumers (engagement by month)

- Engaged company once
- Engaged company in 2 ways
- Engaged company in at least 3 ways
- Ready to buy

Month	Engaged once	2 ways	3+ ways	Ready to buy
Mar-15	74%	13%	11%	2%
Apr-15	59%	28%	10%	3%
May-15	66%	17%	12%	5%
Jun-15	64%	14%	15%	7%
Jul-15	26%	40%	20%	14%

Our new design promotes *substantial engagement* with consumers and has increased the percentage of those ready to buy.

Copyright © 2019 by Steve Shu Consulting

Figure 3.1: An Example of Cohort Measurements

Note that the list above related to behavioral science and innovation considerations is not an exhaustive list. Readers may also want to refer to Chapter 4 which goes a bit further and describes a case for integrating behavioral science into design, innovation, and thinking processes.

Traditional Problem Statements and Behavioral Science Consulting Practices

Probably the most common situations faced by mainstream consulting firms involves solving traditional problem statements. By traditional, I don't mean to imply these problems are easy and can be addressed with cookie-cutter solutions. Rather, in contrast to the *divergent thinking* required for innovation projects (as with the Skunk Works account I provided in the prior section), mainstream consulting generally involves addressing problem statements that have much clearer scopes and boundaries. Traditional problem statements tend to require greater use of both *convergent thinking* and engagement structures which essentially break down the problem statement into smaller parts. For example, traditional problem statements might include:

1. How can we assess to what extent our online shopping experience fosters trust between consumers and our partners? What can we do to enhance our experience?
2. To what extent do our call center agents use healthy communications with consumers from a behavioral science perspective, and how can we readapt and refine our processes to become better?
3. Can we figure out what our competitive strategy is relative to new entrants (who may be applying behavioral science concepts) when providing services to consumers, and whether we should build, buy, partner, monitor, or ignore these companies?
4. How can we quantify the benefit of improving our cost structure relative to bill collection operations, and what can be done from a communications perspective across paper mailings, emails, texting, and outbound calling processes to improve things?
5. Can we assess what we are doing relative to marketing, and see what we can do to modernize

and personalize our approach? How can we improve both engagement and education of consumers and then empower them to take action using behavioral science principles?

One of the clients that I worked for (with colleagues at Digitai, a behavioral science consultancy) had a problem statement closely aligned with item 5 above. Although I've stylized the activity descriptions and timeframes from what was actually done for instructional purposes in this book, there were essentially four workstreams that the client pursued (see Figure 3.2):

- **Behavioral Science Strategy** – Strategy development included assessing current marketing collateral and consumer communications through behavioral lenses (in terms of information, choice, and thinking architecture). We also brought some key vendors to the table that could collaborate with us and modernize the client's consumer engagement experience. An example of one key vendor we brought to the table was Idomoo (idomoo.com), essentially a technology-provider of personalized videos[15] that can be manufactured on-the-fly during a consumer's interaction, such as during a web experience. Videos can be personalized based on both information associated with the individual (such as gender, age, account information) and branching logic (such as based on actions taken by the individual and computerized business rules). The basic idea was to create short, sixty-second videos, with storyboards informed by behavioral science, and then deliver these videos to

---

[15] To get a sense of what personalized videos look like, one can visit the support section of my website at www.InsideNudging.com and explore the links associated with Idomoo. Note that referenced videos are not created by Digitai (unless stated as such), and the videos may not be informed by behavioral science in terms of the storyboard details, visual design, orchestration, and calls to action (if any).

consumers at key touch points to drive behavior change.

- **Technology Strategy** – The workstream associated with technology strategy consisted of efforts that were similar to many other business projects involving technology. The keys were to connect the dots between the behavioral science-based solutions desired today and the first generation technology architecture while maintaining some perspective on the longer-term evolution strategy for future behavioral science interventions. In the client scenario I describe here, the client mostly took responsibility for the technology strategy workstream, although as outside consultants we shared some of our own perspectives.

- **Financial Analysis** – The financial analysis worksteam for the project was also relatively straightforward and essentially included some modeling of benefits and costs for the project initiative. Usually the analysis is a bit of a joint effort, where the client brings in knowledge of the core business while the behavioral science team brings in perspectives on potential effect sizes of various behavioral science interventions (e.g., based on prior lab, field studies, or implementation experience), unknowns, and risks.

- **Solution Development** – The solution development workstream for the project involved a good amount of collaboration between the consulting team and the client, particularly with respect to the front-end activities related to solution design. The reason why this is the case is that since details matter relative to implementing behavioral science interventions most effectively, having the behavioral science team actively involved with requirements development, A/B testing guidance, and design reviews (e.g., during Agile development) is often key. Other areas related to solution development, pilot development, and testing are comparable to non-behavioral science based projects.

Let me summarize some closing thoughts on traditional problem statements and behavioral science consulting practices:
1. Creating engagement structures that are aligned with problem statements is extremely desirable.
2. There can be situations where it is acceptable to have a third-party behavioral science consulting team that is external to the company work on the engagement and interface at key points in the process (for example, in the engagement above the interface points were mostly around strategy and design).
3. A behavioral science team need not be external to the firm. A company can build an Internal Consulting Office. In the Appendix I provide some things to think about when developing this type of organizational model.
4. A company may want to develop a pipeline of candidate, behavioral science-based projects as part of its efforts to work with a third-party consulting firm. Most definitely a company should develop a project pipeline if it builds an Internal Consulting Office.

A consulting engagement structure can help establish the right cadence

Activities	Month 1	Month 2	Month 3
1) Behavioral Science Strategy	←――――――→		
a) Baseline Behavioral Audit	▬▬▬		
b) Solution Workshop	▬▬▬		
c) Competitive Analysis	▬▬▬		
d) Business and Solution Definition		▬▬▬	
2) Technology Strategy	←――――――→		
a) Solution Feasibility	▬▬▬		
b) Architecture and Evolution Path		▬▬▬	
3) Financial Analysis	←――――――→		
a) Financial Modeling	▬▬▬		
b) Baseline Analysis		▬▬▬	
4) Solution Development		←――――――――→	
a) Solution Design		▬▬▬	
b) Solution Development			▬▬▬
c) Pilot Development			▬▬▬
d) Testing			▬▬▬

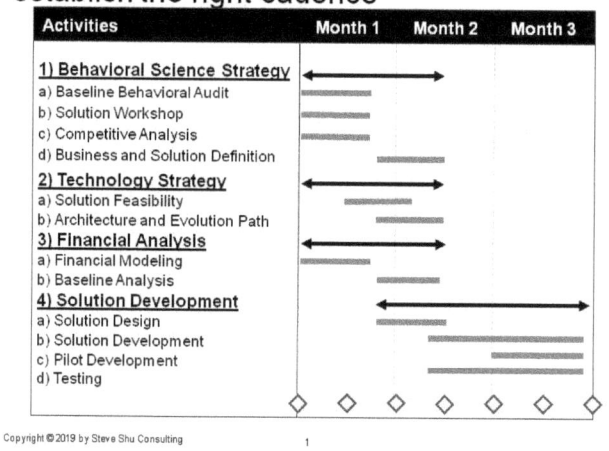

Copyright © 2019 by Steve Shu Consulting

Figure 3.2: An Example of a Consulting Engagement Structure Involving Behavioral Science

Portfolios of Micro-Problem Statements and Consulting Firms Using Focused Behavioral Science Solutions

I've seen, talked, or worked with people from some of the major consulting firms as they start to get their feet wet with behavioral science in a more organized fashion. Their approaches vary in terms of either applying behavioral science principles or using concepts for marketing and thought leadership purposes. In terms of applying (or attempting to apply) behavioral science principles, one area that seems to be emerging with some consultancies is addressing micro-problem statements and using focused solutions. Micro-problem statements tend to be distinguished from other types because the scope is narrow, they reoccur on a regular basis, and to some extent, they can be addressed with a repeatable, common structure. Without evaluating the merit of micro-problem statements and focused solutions, anecdotal examples include:

1. **Website information architecture problem statement:** We are thinking about how our website displays information. Should we display monthly or annual amounts? Should we display percentages?

Focused solution: Companies are building widgets to enable either itself or customers to toggle between the two views based on business rules.

2. **Website choice architecture problem statement:** The goal of our website is to maximize revenue. When we display search results to users, how should we optimize the display of choices so as to meet our goals of maximizing revenue?

   Focused solution: Companies are building sorting and filtering engines that are dynamically configured based on business rules that balance the goals of users and the company.

3. **Preference construction problem statement:** Since some shoppers don't really know their preferences, can we build an engine that infers a shopper's preferences from some hypothetical choices they make?

   Focused solution: Companies are developing engines analogous to the swiping interface of the Tinder app and side-by-side choice selection between two products (e.g., conjoint analysis) as the backbone to a digital experience.

4. **Dynamic choice and process architecture problem statement:** When people buy different items (say a new mobile phone versus new computer), people have very different processes for constructing their preferences. Can we build customized choice engines by product class?

   Focused solution: Some are building engines that work like Mad Libs (www.madlibs.com), where people fill-in the blanks as they build their own story about purchasing a new phone, computer, or other emotionally-involved item.

Note that my sense is that the focused solutions emerging from consulting firms are generally not applied right off-the-shelf. For example, there may be a library of base functionality that might need to be licensed and customized for each client. And the commercial arrangements between the consulting firm and clients probably vary as well (e.g., provided via software as a service or managed services models). As a consultant from one of the big strategy firms told me, when these firms integrate behavioral science, they often gravitate toward identifying the oldest, core problems in behavioral science field and then applying solutions thousands of times over.[16]

I offer some closing thoughts on micro-problem statements and focused behavioral science solutions:

- Some micro-problem statements can have big implications for the bottom line. Others might be required simply for good hygiene and to ensure design is deliberate and not accidental. Regardless, context is important for assessing potential impact.
- Some micro-problem statements might turn out to be very repeatable and generalizable, and getting smarter in this area seems like a good aspiration for organizations dedicated to continuous improvement.
- Creating software solutions for these micro-problem statements is an extremely formative area, and we will likely see more activity in the future. Companies should consider looking at what the consulting firms are doing in this domain. They

---

[16] Some consulting firms (such as the IBMs and Accentures of the world) and companies have been moving in the direction of using big data and building significant capabilities around behavioral models. These models often involve analyzing the behavior of individuals (and potentially peers) and predicting each individual's likely next behavior. These prediction models may then be used by the company to determine the most appropriate messaging and interventions to use when next communicating and interacting with the individual.

should also look at startups and the technology firms involved with big data and large consumer bases.

Key Takeaways

I began this chapter with a story illustrating that consultants may be both change agents and signs of change. Whether your company uses consultants or not, a lot can be learned from how consultants approach problems. Consulting is centered around problem statements and projects:

- For extremely ambitious problem statements, consider an approach motivated by Skunk Works.

- For traditional problem statements, see if you can adopt the approach that consulting firms use by defining a compelling engagement structure.

- For micro-problem statements, be on the lookout for repeatable patterns, and additionally seek inspiration from outside your company.

4
LOOK AT PROBLEMS HOLISTICALLY AND BUILD AN INNOVATION CAPABILITY

From an app on your smartphone you are about to order lunch to be delivered by a peer-to-peer car service (similar to Uber). From the time you place your order, the car service can deliver lunch to your doorstep in about three to ten minutes. Consider the following scenarios:

Scenario 1: It is the year 2015, and nearing the end of your order, you are given the choice of two desserts: an awesome chocolate brownie or a yummy oatmeal raisin cookie. In small font, but only appearing after five seconds if you haven't chosen any dessert, an option will appear to decline dessert altogether.

Scenario 2: It is the year 2018, and nearing the end of your order, you place an order for an awesome chocolate brownie. Before you can finalize your order:

1. The app provides a notice that the brownie is outside of the calorie budget you have set up in the health app and asks you if you'd rather decline the chocolate brownie.
2. When you decide not to decline the brownie after the first notice, the app reminds you that you are meeting with a colleague tonight and that you may

want to save your calories for later since the restaurant serves an awesome crème brûlée (for equal calories to the brownie). And based on your past ratings, you are much more likely to enjoy the crème brûlée.
3. If you like, the app can even reserve your dessert for tonight and arrange a car to transport you to and from the restaurant. (Better outcomes for you based on your priorities, and more money for the service provider.)

Take a moment to think about what was different about Scenario 1 and 2. In which of the scenarios did the app tap into faster thinking to a greater extent? In which of the two scenarios did the app help you to slow down and think through more tradeoffs? In which of these two scenarios did you trust the app more?

The Scenario 1 app taps into faster thinking. It puts two choices of dessert in front of you, presumes that you want one of them, and delays your ability to opt-out of any dessert. The app practically prods you into selecting a dessert.

While the Scenario 2 app may not have completely tapped into your deep, reflective thinking, it probably did slow your thinking down a bit. The app gave you a series of things to think about; a type of process architecture to help guide you with preference formation and decision-making. And while I'm not sure how you felt about the app in Scenario 1 versus Scenario 2 in terms of trust, your perceived relationship to the app in Scenario 1 versus 2 likely differed. Maybe the app in Scenario 1 was like a bully, pushing you around. Maybe the app in Scenario 2 was more like an advisor or friend.

In this chapter, I'd like to explore a few things:
1) Looking at problems more holistically.
2) Going beyond information and choice architecture to look at process architecture (and potentially engaging slower thinking).
3) Examining meaning-driven innovation (and examining relationships).

A Look at the Retirement Goal Planning System

After the Save More Tomorrow work discussed in Chapter

2 had been incubated, in 2014 the Allianz Global Investors Center for Behavioral Finance embarked on another challenging area. Namely, how could we begin to address behavioral judgment and decision-making issues associated with those approaching or already in retirement? One element of the approach included developing thought leadership content and tools. By May of 2015, a new book, *Thinking Smarter*, was released to the public along with a free companion app, called the Retirement Goal Planning System. More info on the app can be found at www.RetirementGoalPlanningSystem.com (Benartzi and Lewin 2015).

In order to better understand this app, we first need to take a more holistic look at some of the challenges of the retirement journey. Such an examination will shed more light on the behavioral angle of process architecture (which I have alluded to previously but haven't explored in depth). At a high-level, I see a number of macro-level issues:

- **People really don't like retirement planning** – Some people may love to plan vacations, but retirement as a life event requires life readjustments, which creates stress (including emotional stress). And stress is partly associated with the onset of illness. To help put things in context, the Social Readjustment Rating Scale provides a rough, relative rating of the amount of stress experienced for various life events. The Social Readjustment Rating Scale for adults roughly rates retirement less stressful than going to jail but more than pregnancy or death of a close friend (Holmes and Rahe 1967).
- **Retirement planning is inherently a challenging problem** - It involves a long horizon with lots of thinking traps, risks, and uncertainties[17]. Without going into a lot of analysis

---

[17] Note that the academic literature has nuanced terms related to risk, unknown unknowns, and the like. To address a broader audience, I'll use the terms risk and uncertainty somewhat loosely. That said, two notable angles to the situation we

here, it is very difficult to foresee what one's life might be like in ten, twenty, or even fifty years or more. Imagine a person that is sixty years old and might live to or past one hundred and ten years old. It is a hard planning problem to think about.

- **From a behavioral perspective, the saving for retirement problem is much easier than the retirement spending problem** – The former problem is sometimes referred to as the accumulation problem. That is, how does one save enough money for retirement? Although a person's means to save can clearly be an issue, as the Save More Tomorrow research indicated (in Chapter 2 and Figure 2.4), employees of similar means can end up saving vastly different amounts simply by changing the behavioral architecture that employees face. On the other hand, once one has retired, the retirement spending problem comes into focus, sometimes referred to as the decumulation problem. How does one determine how much wealth to use over time (i.e., decumulate wealth) now that income from a job may no longer exist? Addressing the accumulation problem from a behavioral perspective is much easier (See Figure

---

address in this chapter include 1) risk analysis relative to longevity, pre-retirement investment returns, and stochastic health outcomes, and 2) changes in cognitive ability over one's life. Interested readers should consult the original sources. For angle 1, depending upon what income quartile one lands in, Employee Benefits Research Institute essentially found that winning the longevity or losing the health outcomes roll of the die can wipe out a person's retirement readiness prospects (VanDerhei 2014). For angle 2, those interested in learning more about how cognitive ability increases relative to vocabulary from one's twenties to early retirement and the seventies (and then slightly declines on average) but decreases in terms of speed, reasoning, and memory perspectives from one's twenties, one foundational source includes work by Timothy Salthouse (Salthouse 2004).

4.1). Furthermore, solving the decumulation problem cannot be done by simply manipulating choice and information architecture. People are a lot more diverse later in life (e.g., some have good genetics and will likely live very long, others may be in poor health and have a different planning horizon) and those elements of heterogeneity have a large impact on determining which decisions are optimal.

- **Customer experience needs to evolve** – During my observation of the courtship between various retirees and wealth management advisors (both independent ones and those as part of larger firms), it was not uncommon to run into situations where one party was from Mars and the other was from Venus. Notable themes included some retirees 1) not feeling listened to by the advisor, 2) getting lost in explanations of complex investment analyses prepared by the advisor, and 3) questioning whether the recommendations prepared were really customized for the retiree's needs. See Figure 4.2 for some paraphrased comments by retirees.

The complexity of decumulation pales that of accumulation. *(For illustrative, educational purposes only)*

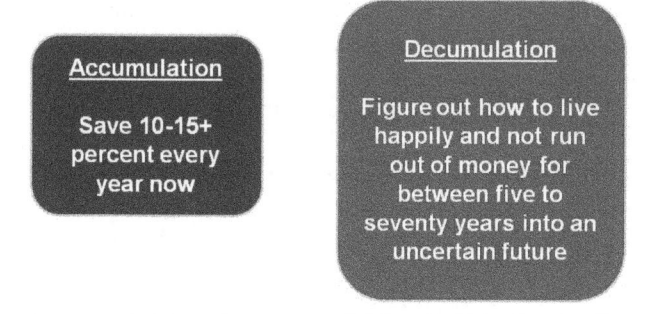

Accumulation

Save 10-15+ percent every year now

Decumulation

Figure out how to live happily and not run out of money for between five to seventy years into an uncertain future

Copyright © 2019 by Steve Shu Consulting

Figure 4.1: The Retirement Challenge

Advisors are from Mars, and retirees are from Venus.

"The advisor just talked about himself and didn't listen to my needs."

"I don't see how the financial plan the advisor recommend to me differs from what he'd recommend to my son."

"The advisor showed me fifty some pages of financial information and made me feel stupid."

Copyright © 2019 by Steve Shu Consulting

Figure 4.2: Some Reasons Why the Relationship Between Advisors and Retirees Needs to Change

Exploring Goals

In order to develop an effective business initiative that starts to address some of these issues, a company should really look at the first part of the Behavioral GRIT™ framework. Namely, a company should actively explore and vet its understanding of goals for various constituents. These activities may take time and effort, involve various discussions and meetings between people within and outside the company, and require some field research. In the case of Allianz Global Investors, there were three perspectives to examine:

1. **What are the company goals, and how can the company develop a unique approach to address those goals?** As described in Chapter 2, Allianz Global Investors Center for Behavioral Finance was established with the goal of turning academic insights into actionable ideas and practical tools. Since the decumulation challenge is quite complex (as described earlier), the Center needed to tackle a more narrowly-scoped problem at the front end for retirees nearing or at

retirement. Goals were to help business partners and retirees in general with retirement planning (as opposed to pushing products). The opportunity was to develop a unique approach that applied behavioral finance concepts and would elevate the prominence of Allianz Global Investors as a whole with its business partners.

2. **How can the company help advisors?** The goals of advisors in the wealth management space are to help retirees and make money. They generally do this through developing relationships with individual retirees, whether the advisor works as part of larger firm or is independent. How these advisors make money varies, such as via fixed fees for consultation or a percentage of assets managed. The goals of advisors also extend beyond making money. For example, they may help retirees think about strategies for Social Security claiming or managing tax considerations.

3. **How can the company help retirees?** In this case, it is necessary for both advisors to help retirees and retirees to be able to help themselves. The goals of retirees include needing to have enough money to last in retirement and achieving their life and legacy aspirations. So the company could facilitate this by providing behavioral finance tools and content to both advisors and retirees. And as we'll see in a moment, a key aspect would be to provide a tool that uses process architecture (or "thinking architecture" as coined in the *Thinking Smarter* book), to help retirees think more slowly, broadly, and deeply, potentially in conjunction with their advisor.

Connecting in Research

Research is the next area of the Behavioral GRIT™ framework. The business initiative involved researching and identifying (through a mixture of primary and secondary research) the behavioral obstacles that retirees encounter during the retirement planning process. These obstacles

include (Benartzi and Lewin 2015):
1. Focusing on alternatives versus goals.
2. Memory recall limitations.
3. Tradeoff avoidance (e.g., cognitive and emotional).
4. Focusing on one future versus considering risk.
5. Forecasting limitations.
6. Failing to seek input from others.
7. Anchoring and status quo bias.

Note that although I've outlined the behavioral obstacles in a tidy list here, the discovery and research process can be quite involved.

The aspect of identifying behavioral obstacles is an important one. Why? The process feeds the behavioral solution process. And if we look at the case of the behavioral obstacles listed above, it's not hard to imagine why it would be impossible to give retirees information and a simple set of choices to overcome the obstacles. Solutions will need to go further and consider process architecture, in this case giving the retiree some thinking tools. This process architecture is codified into a 7-step process that is based on behavioral science and could be conducted on a Apple iPad (using the Retirement Goal Planning System app) by a retiree, with or without the assistance of a financial advisor (Allianz Global Investors Center for Behavioral Finance 2015). The seven steps are:

1. Identify Your Goals.
2. Discover Blind Spots.
3. Prioritize Your Goals.
4. Think Beyond One Future.
5. Recognize the Limits of Forecasting.
6. Consider the Perspectives of Others.
7. Reprioritize Goals.

To give you a concrete example of how some of these steps are implemented in the app, first consider step 3 which covers prioritizing goals. Prioritizing goals is an inherently challenging problem, sometimes from both cognitive complexity and emotional perspectives. And for most people facing retirement, prioritization is needed simply because resources are limited (e.g., financial). So by the time retirees have gone through the first two steps of the process, which help to ensure we are considering all of the goals that are important to them, we then ask them in step 3 to prioritize their goals using a "prioritization board" of sorts. Goals like "Financial Independence" and "Ending Life with Dignity" are represented as tiles. Retirees then arrange goals on the prioritization board with three spots for identifying the most important, four spots for moderately important, and five spots for least important. See Figure 4.3.

Figure 4.3: Screenshot of Step 3 of the Retirement Goal Planning System App

As another example of how some of the steps are implemented in the app, consider step 4 which helps retirees to think beyond one future. More specifically, this step helps retirees overcome the behavioral obstacle of failing to think about risk and potential good and bad outcomes. From a behavioral perspective, people tend to make the error of thinking about the future as one (probable) outcome. So in step 4 we ask people to think about both good and bad outcomes. And there's an additional twist. We employ a psychological tool of prospective hindsight (Mitchell, Russo and Pennington 1989) to help one think about outcomes at different ends of the spectrum. Prospective hindsight takes advantage of the scientific observation that people have a harder time enumerating potential details if asked to *forecast* events. So instead of asking people to forecast events, we ask them to enumerate details about the future as if a particular future event has already happened. For example, in Figure 4.4. we instruct the retiree to "Imagine it is 20 years from now. What would your life *have been like* if things went well?" When it comes to the human mind, looking backward is easier even if it is really only in your mind. See Figures 4.4 and 4.5 for how we implemented step 4 in two subparts.

Step 4a

Imagine Your Retirement If Things Went Well

Imagine it is 20 years from now. What would your life have been like if things went well? How would you describe this situation in terms of your goals? Take a few minutes to describe what your life would have been like. You can do this verbally with your advisor or spouse, or jot down what comes to mind.

When you are done, click continue.

Source: Allianz Global Investors Center for Behavioral Finance 2015

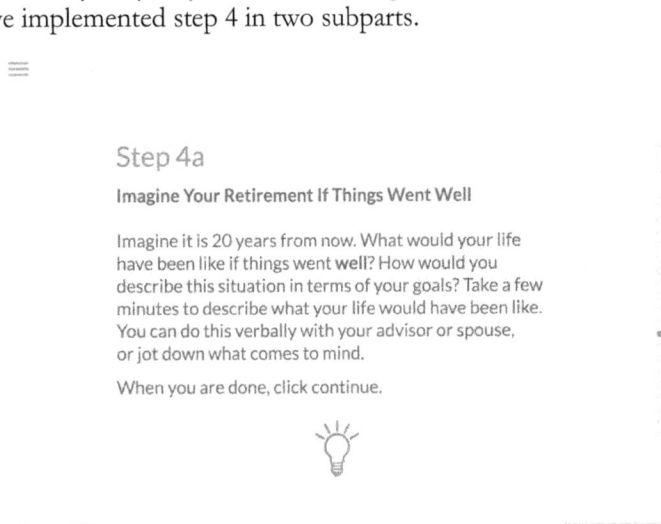

Figure 4.4: Screenshot of Step 4a of the Retirement Goal Planning System App (Uses Prospective Hindsight)

Once a retiree has prioritized their goals using the Retirement Goal Planning System, they can then think about the next steps, say with an advisor. For example, if the retiree rated the goal of Financial Independence as important, they could consider a retirement strategy like Claim More Tomorrow (Benartzi and Lewin 2015), a strategy that involves deferring the claiming of Social Security benefits until a later date in order to receive higher future benefit payments (Shoven and Slavov March 2013). On the other hand, if the retiree rated the goal of Giving Back as important, they could consider using money and time to help others.

Step 4b

Imagine Your Retirement If Things Went Badly

Now imagine it's 20 years from now but things went badly. What would your life have been like? How would you describe this situation in terms of your goals? Take a few minutes to describe verbally or in writing, what your life would have been like in this scenario.

When you are done, click continue.

Source: Allianz Global Investors Center for Behavioral Finance 2015

Figure 4.5: Screenshot of Step 4b of the Retirement Goal Planning System App (Uses Prospective Hindsight)

Let's summarize how the research was connected in this case. We used the research to help define the problem statement we wanted to tackle, namely retirement planning. We used research to help us identify key obstacles that are encountered during the process of retirement planning, which in turn helped us to think about solutions informed by behavioral science. Similar to the PlanSuccess case in Chapter 2 where a 3x3 framework relates behavioral obstacles with desired outcomes and solutions (mostly in the choice and information architecture realms), we essentially have a 7x1 framework here. That is, the Retirement Goal Planning System covers seven primary obstacles and a matching set of seven solutions (i.e, steps organized into a process architecture) based on behavioral science.

Examining Innovation

I have always found the topic of innovation to be exciting. There are many good sources for perspectives, philosophies, and processes on innovation. A favorite of mine is the book *Blue Ocean Strategy* (Kim and Mauborgne 2005), which essentially focuses on creating new opportunities in a "blue ocean" through encouraging strategists and designers to think differently, often bucking traditional assumptions in an industry. Bucking traditional assumptions might look like striving to design an airline that competes with the cost of taxis or developing circuses that neither use clowns nor feature attractions. The Blue Ocean Strategy approach is contrasted with traditional competitive strategy approaches (e.g., Michael Porter's Five Forces) where the competitive space is taken more as a given condition, and thus, presumably constrains thinking. The Blue Ocean Strategy argument is essentially that if a company doesn't define the space that they want to play in, then they are playing in a space that others have defined. Such companies are essentially operating in a space where sharks feed, an undesirable "red ocean" filled by the blood of competition. The blue ocean is unexplored and wide open for the taking. I also like a lot of the work by the famous design firm IDEO (www.ideo.com), especially regarding some of their process thinking around innovation. One can also look for inspiration a bit further from the traditional, corporate tree. Companies who apply principles from improv theater (like the concept of "Yes, and") can also benefit from the creativity unlocked by trained, smart people working together.

In terms of the topic of innovation in this book, I'd like to focus more narrowly. In particular, one special perspective comes from Roberto Verganti, who coined the term, "Design-Driven Innovation." He has an excellent book under the same name (Verganti 2009). For our purposes I'd like to re-coin some of Verganti's thinking under the moniker of "Meaning-Driven Innovation." I see his framing of design around "meanings" as being rather unique yet very compatible with the field of behavioral science.

So what does it mean to center design around meanings? What is meaning-driven innovation? Meaning-driven innovation is essentially about changing both the interpretations by and relationships of people through design.

Meaning-driven innovation can be viewed in contrast to innovation driven primarily by technological advances. The classic case that Verganti highlights in his book is the case of the Nintendo Wii in 2006 (Verganti 2009). Here's the short story version of what happened. Sony and Microsoft essentially dominated the video game console space with the PlayStation 3 and Xbox 360, respectively. These incumbent consoles primarily relied on technological advances with faster performance and improved graphics to drive product advances. Then essentially out of nowhere and with a meteoric rise came the Nintendo Wii. The Nintendo Wii didn't rely on high resolution graphics or cutting-edge performance. Nintendo created game that provided physical entertainment and a way for people to socialize through gaming. Sure the Nintendo Wii leveraged advances in technology; some of the Nintendo gaming aspects such as gesture-based controls were enabled through new technology and use of accelerometers in the hand controllers. But Nintendo changed the industry space by changing the meaning of gaming. The Nintendo Wii provided a physical and social entertainment escape for people of all ages. And the design made gaming broadly accessible and easy to use. The Nintendo Wii was the first video game I ever saw brought widely into elementary schools, retirement homes, and different cross-sections of human life.

Whether a product is something less mainstream like Artemide's Yang lamp that makes you feel better (versus other lamps which simple provide illumination), or mainstream, such as Apple's iPod that provided a breakthrough way to discover, purchase, and enjoy music (versus the Walkman and other predecessors that provided portable access), the opportunity to pursue meaning-driven innovation is tremendous. For the Retirement Goal Planning System, we sought to change the traditional relationship between financial advisors and retirees. The traditional meaning or relationship between advisors and retirees has been to focus on the 3Fs, which are fees, funds, and fiduciary responsibility. While those aspects of the advisor-retiree relationship are important, we wanted to provide advisors a tool that enabled them to learn more about a retiree's goals. We wanted to enable a process that would provide deeper opportunities for both parties to think more slowly, broadly, and deeply. In concept, this setup would enable skilled advisors to provide more tailored advice. We envisioned a market where some advisors evolved into trusted advisors, perhaps even incorporating aspects of life coaches and cover more than just traditional financial support. In

Figure 4.6 you can see how our strategy leverages behavioral science in an effort to change the meaning of the financial advisor.

Approach Summary: Use behavioral science as part of meaning-driven innovation.

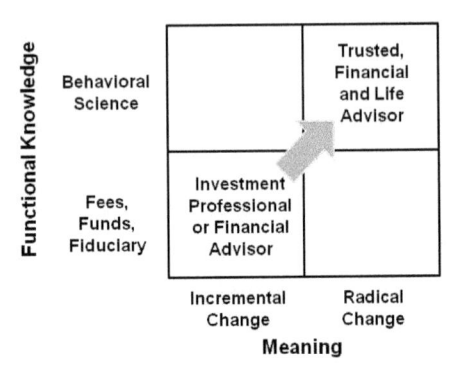

Figure 4.6: The Retirement Goal Planning System Aspires to Change the Meaning of the Relationships of Financial Advisors

As a final thought on the search to change and evolve meanings, another favorite source of inspiration for me is the book by Gerald and Lindsay Zaltman, *Marketing Metaphoria* (Zaltman and Zaltman 2008), which puts forth the concept of deep metaphors. Deep metaphors encapsulate the core structure of what people hear, think, say, and do. So for example, after conducting interviews, the authors found the metaphor theme of "money is like a liquid" from surface metaphor sayings like, "Money runs through his fingers" or "Don't pour your money down the drain." The metaphor theme of "money is like a liquid" was then generalized to the deep metaphor of Resource.

The authors extracted seven deep metaphors based on more than 12,000 interviews in over 30 countries related to numerous products and services. These metaphors are:
1. Balance
2. Transformation
3. Journey

4. Container
5. Connection
6. Resource
7. Control

If I had to characterize a predominant deep metaphor related to the Retirement Goal Planning System, it would be that of Connection. We try to change the way a retiree relates to their future self and their advisor through using a tool that helps the parties think deeply about who they are and what really matters.

A Peek at Testing

Testing is the final business area of the Behavioral GRIT™ framework. In this section, I'd like to briefly touch on two aspects that were core to the creation of the Retirement Goal Planning System. The first has to do with core testing needs, and the second has to do with testing structure.

With respect to first, if we take a step back from the Retirement Goal Planning System, the core testing needs were around design. Earlier in this chapter, I alluded to the notion that advisors are from Mars, and retirees are from Venus (Figure 4.2). This observation primarily came about through ethnographic research where we went into the field and observed advisors and retirees from a third-party, fly-on-the-wall perspective and didn't interfere with the way current business was done between the parties. Naturally, when it came to developing our tools and content, we did testing by going back to some of these advisors and retirees to get them to respond to our proposed designs and "test out our wares," so to speak. As part of an agile process, we refined our designs based on that type of testing.

To shed more light on the second aspect of the testing structure, our approach could also have included laboratory work. Laboratory work often provides a researcher with an opportunity to perform more highly-controlled evaluation of an intervention's effectiveness. However, it was going to be difficult to get our core constituents into a lab. And we needed to reach more advisors and retirees than could be practically reached through ethnographic observation settings, where we needed permission from both advisors and retirees to shadow them throughout the courting process. To make a long story short, we went with variants of surveys, phone interviews, and one-on-one interviews to get more insights from individuals on retirement planning. Some of these activities served as either background research or as a way to test the completeness of our design (e.g., checking if we were missing any retirement goals in our master set of goal tiles for the 7-step system). This balance between field testing and controlled lab testing illustrates some of the tradeoffs that come with different testing methods, and is a key reason why both approaches add value.

Key Takeaways

- **Look at the problem holistically** – An examination of any core research and a deep introspection of goals for various constituents are key. As part of that effort, I often find it important to continuously articulate and rearticulate the understanding of goals and the problem statement throughout an initiative. For the Retirement Goal Planning System, during our examination of the research and constituent goals, we not only found a number of unaddressed behavioral obstacles facing retirees, but also found big disconnects in the communications between financial advisors and retirees.

- **Consider process architecture as another available tool** – Sometimes we discover that the behavioral obstacles that people face cannot be overcome simply by changing the choice and information architecture, and process architecture might be a consideration. For the Retirement Goal Planning System, we encouraged people to slow down their thinking, think more broadly, and think more deeply through the use of a 7-step system (i.e., process architecture). Process architecture approaches can be powerful. David Halpern relates a case where his team essentially facilitated a process architecture to help jobseekers think about their job search, which resulted an increase from 51% to 60% of jobseekers at 13 weeks to be off of benefits (Halpern 2015).

- **Think about innovation philosophy, and consider meaning-driven innovation** – Behavioral science includes acquiring a better understanding of how people behave. And so I view the field as very compatible with meaning-driven innovation which focuses on interpretations by and relationships between people. While the innovation process for the Retirement Goal Planning System largely involved getting smart people into a room together, factoring in research, and networking to assimilate perspectives from various corners of the industry, different processes could have been used. That said, the philosophy of meaning-driven innovation – changing the relationship of the financial advisor to the retiree through a Connection deep metaphor[18] – was key.

---

[18] I should note that the use of meaning-driven innovation and deep metaphors is mostly a post-hoc explanation of what happened in the case of the Retirement Goal Planning System. That said, these principles guide my thinking, and I try to use these concepts wherever sensible.

5
NUDGE PSYCHE AND EXPLORING ETHICS

In January 2012, the Core Data Science Team at Facebook and researchers at Cornell University conducted a experiment involving just shy of 700,000 Facebook users (Kramer, Guillory and Hancock 2014). A key question that the team wanted to answer through this "mood study" was assessing to what extent emotions could be transferred via the social network without user awareness. The experiment would involve manipulating a user's news feed and the amount of positive or negative emotional content within that feed. They then wanted to see whether varying levels of exposure would result in that end user posting more positive or negative content.

The upshot was that when a user was exposed to more positive content, the user tended to post more positive content. Conversely, when a user was exposed to more negative content, the user tended to post more negative content. Voila. While the net effect sizes of the manipulations were small, the field experiment provided evidence of emotional contagion via social networks.

The study was published in June 2014, and the context and reaction of the public was captured in the title of a New York Times article, which read "Facebook Tinkers With Users'

Emotions in News Feed Experiment, Stirring Outcry." The first line of the article reads, "To Facebook, we are all lab rats." (Goel 2014)

The reactions to Facebook's mood study included a wide range of perspectives. In their own defense, Facebook claimed that users consent (essentially a "blanket" consent) to these types of manipulations through agreeing to its terms of service (Goel 2014), although the Proceedings of the National Academy of Sciences (PNAS) issued a rare editorial expression of concern about potential inconsistencies with principles of informed consent and ability for users to opt-out of the experiment (Verma 2014).

According to the Wall Street Journal (Krishna 2014), Cheryl Sandberg, Facebook's COO said:

"This was part of ongoing research companies do to test different products, and that was what it was; it was poorly communicated."

In contrast, there were passionate negative reactions from users, as could be seen in the comments section of the same article where Survivor wrote:

"I am a survivor of long term domestic abuse, and I have PTSD. Even the thought that someone may have manipulated my emotional state sickens me. And, having lived with a sociopath for most of my adult life, your response to what really was a terrible decision that violated your users most basic rights mimics the behaviors of the monster with whom I used to live: refusing to acknowledge responsibility for your actions…You never truly will know the effect your decision had. And your organization should be punished for its actions."

While we're on the topic of Facebook, and as food for thought, I'd like to offer a figure adapted from *The Washington Post* which was actually captioned, "Americans Trust IRS and NSA More than Facebook and Google to Protect Privacy" (Fung 2013). We'll revisit the role of trust later in this chapter, since trust plays an important role with respect to the acceptability of nudges.

Facebook tends not to score well on trust measures

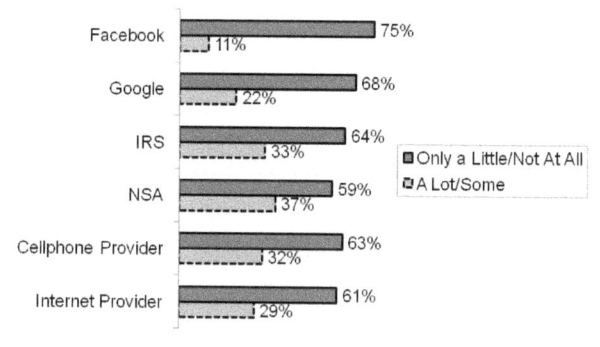

Organization	Only a Little/Not At All	A Lot/Some
Facebook	75%	11%
Google	68%	22%
IRS	64%	33%
NSA	59%	37%
Cellphone Provider	63%	32%
Internet Provider	61%	29%

Source: Fung, Brian. "Facebook wants to know if you trust it. But it's keeping all the answers to itself." *The Washington Post.* December 31, 2013. https://www.washingtonpost.com/news/the-switch/wp/2013/12/31/facebook-wants-to-know-if-you-trust-it-but-its-keeping-all-the-answers-to-itself/ (accessed September 16, 2015).
Copyright © 2019 by Steve Shu Consulting

Figure 5.1: To What Extent Do People Trust These Organizations?

Hot on the heels of the Facebook mood study fiasco, one month later in July 2014 OkCupid, an online dating site, became the center of attention for another case study on ethics. Christian Rudder posted on the OkCupid blog, "We Experiment On Human Beings!" Christian shared some interesting statistics that measured the "A/B testing" effects of blind courtship and dates (where no photos of daters were shared) versus regular courtship and dates (where dater photos were shared). But somewhat more controversially, he also shared some A/B testing data where some daters were told untruths (i.e., lies) about how compatible they were (Rudder 2014). For example, whereas OkCupid's algorithms may have assessed two potential daters match compatibility at 30%, in the test some daters were instead told a lie that they had a match compatibility 90%. The variable effects of actual match compatibility versus what people were told is reflected in the chart below.

OkCupid study shows both match compatibility and power of suggestion affect dating conversations

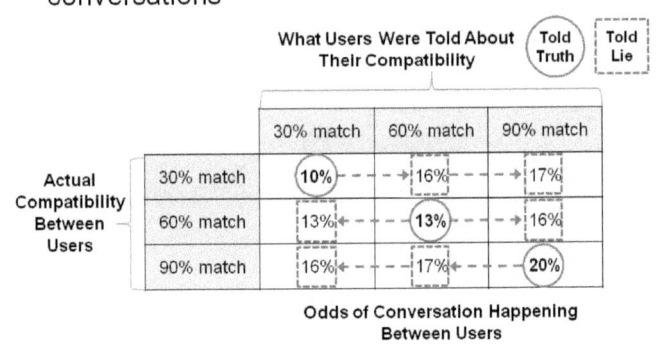

		\multicolumn{3}{c}{What Users Were Told About Their Compatibility (Told Truth / Told Lie)}
		30% match	60% match	90% match
Actual Compatibility Between Users	30% match	10%	16%	17%
	60% match	13%	13%	16%
	90% match	16%	17%	20%

Odds of Conversation Happening Between Users

Adapted from source: http://blog.okcupid.com/index.php/we-experiment-on-human-beings (accessed September 17, 2015)
Copyright © 2019 by Steve Shu Consulting

Figure 5.2: What Happened When OKCupid Told Users Lies About Their Compatibility

When actual match compatibility was 30% and the users were told the truth that their match compatibility was also 30% (upper left corner of the chart), then 10% of the time single messages turned into a conversation between the users (defined as an exchange of four messages). On the other hand, if actual match compatibility was 30% and users were told a lie that their match compatibility was instead 90% (upper right corner of the chart), then the percentage increased and 17% of the time single messages turned into a conversation between the users.

A Huffington Post article by Joseph Farrell led with the title, "Why OKCupid's 'Experiments' Were Worse Than Facebook's" (Farrell 2014). While Christian Rudder at OkCupid essentially claims that as users of the Internet we are all part of hundreds of experiments or A/B tests at any given time, Joseph Farrell expressed things more carefully. He agreed with A/B testing but had a different take on OkCupid's specific approach by writing, "…OkCupid simply lied, falsifying their results and intentionally mismatching people."

Accidental Versus Deliberate Ethics: Nudge Design and Nudgee Attitudes

In Chapter 1, I introduced the notion that when we view the world through behavioral lenses, then it follows that we either approach design from an accidental or deliberate perspective. The same applies to design and ethics. We should be conscious of our design, as choices indirectly reflect ethics.

Consider the following examples related to morality, and rate how acceptable you find each behavior on scale of 1 (not at all acceptable) to 7 (extremely acceptable):

1) While hunting, a person beats a seal over the head to death.

2) When a parent, whose children have grown and married, passes away, the married son claims most of the property and the married daughter claims little.

3) A salesperson sells products for a financial services firm and has done so for many years. The firm treats the salesperson very well in both good and bad times. A relative of the salesperson needs a recommendation for a product and the salesperson offers their company's product over another company's product even though the other company's product is better for the relative.

4) A next generation crowdfunding site wants to have an ad campaign that depicts teenagers rebelling against teachers, as well as parents encouraging teenagers to skip higher education and instead pursue entrepreneurial dreams while they are still young.

5) To maximize competitive differentiation while apparently staying within the boundaries of the law, an auto manufacturer admits to implementing a questionable design feature. When the car is being tested for emissions the car switches into a low-emissions mode that applies only to testing situations and not normal driving conditions.

Note: Examples #1 and #2 are adapted from Jonathan Haidt's book, *The Righteous Mind*, a terrific popular science book that touches on moral psychology (Haidt 2013). Example #5 is loosely based on events with Volkswagen in late 2015 (Hotten 2015).

Different people will view the acceptability of each situation differently. For example, in example #1, you may view the notion of harm differently whether it applies to humans or animals. And your frame of reference for morality may depend on where you grew up and live. If you were born and live in Canada, Norway, or Russia, you might tend to find the behavior in example #1 more acceptable. If you are from the United States you might find the behavior in example #2 less acceptable than if you are from India, due to the way people in these cultures view the morality of fairness in inheritance. Example #3 illustrates tensions that can arise regarding loyalty, and example #4 may invoke a number of feelings regarding how you feel about either authority or liberty. Finally, example #5 appears to trigger feelings depending on how you view the foundational dimension of sanctity (in this case, relative to degradation of the environment and harmful emissions).

So while I might have my own perspectives on what is right or wrong and how to implement nudges, I can't tell you what is right or wrong for your ideology or situation. But I can offer a way to help think about it by highlighting some key perspectives for looking at things.

I call this way of thinking Nudge Psyche, and it is a checklist of things to think about so that you can be deliberate about how you approach nudge design and ethics. It attempts to help design by thinking about things from two broad perspectives: nudge design and nudgee attitudes. For nudge design, one should think about goals, controllability, and influence type. For nudgee attitudes, one should think about trust, fairness, and acceptability. See the Figure 5.3.

Nudge Psyche draws from a variety of research literatures including decision science, medical ethics, government, organizational behavior, behavioral science, and moral psychology. Let's take a closer look at the six areas of the Nudge Psyche checklist.

Nudge Psyche Checklist

Nudge Design			Nudgee Attitudes		
1. Goals	2. Controllability	3. Influence Type	4. Trust	5. Fairness	6. Acceptability
• Individual • Company	• Substantial Non-control • Resistability Versus Easy Resistance • System 1 • System 2	• Rational Persuasion • "Narrow" Nudge • Constructed Preferences • Incentive • Disincentive • Behavioral Prod • Coercion • Compulsion • Choice Elimination	• Goal Alignment • Ownership (e.g., psych)	• Procedural Justice • Distributive Justice • Interpersonal Justice • Informational Justice	• Positive Frames • Demonstrate Effectiveness (Experienced, Hypothetical) • Effectiveness of Others Over Self • Highlighting Intentions (e.g., Sustainability, Health) • Social Dominance Orientation (or Moral Foundations Theory)

Copyright © 2019 by Steve Shu Consulting

Figure 5.3: Use the Nudge Psyche Checklist to Treat Nudge Design and Ethics Deliberately

Area 1: Examine Constituent Goals

In Chapter 2, I relate a behavioral finance case where a company strongly aligns its goals with individuals and partners. More generally, while the degree of alignment depends partially on the structure of the problem at hand (unless the problem is reframed), nudge designers should examine the goals of each constituent. The Nudge Psyche checklist identifies companies and individuals as two perspectives from which to examine things. However, additional perspectives may also apply.

To recap, the behavioral finance case in Chapter 2 involves the following goals (not exhaustive):

- Company wants the industry to view it as a thought leader with unique and substantial contributions to doing good.
- Individual employees want to maximize their near-term interests and opportunities (e.g., living life today, getting their fair share) and balance long-term interests (e.g., having enough to retire on).
- Employers want to maximize the effectiveness of their budgets and help individuals they employ to

join employer retirement plans, save enough, and invest wisely.
- Company partners want a differentiated way to approach and help employers (and the employer's employees).

I described in Chapter 2 how the company chose to address these goals, with some key elements being establishing a market-leading presence in behavioral finance, forming a point of view as to what outcomes would be best for employees and employers, and developing a framework that partners could use with employers to develop customized solutions.

What about the case with Facebook at the beginning of this chapter? Consider the following types of questions:
- What goals does Facebook have in terms of people using the site? In terms of making money? In terms of learning what works and doesn't work on their site?
- To what extent does Facebook make money from individuals? From advertisers? Other?
- What goals do individuals have in terms of feeling connected? Being the center of attention? Being entertained? Learning? Feeling safe?

Since other authors have more exhaustively covered goal-based approaches, I don't intend in this book to provide a full methodology for identifying fundamental versus other goals. Readers may be interested in referencing work in the decision sciences area, such as *Value Focused Thinking* by Ralph Keeney (Keeney 1996). Useful tools from that book, like asking yourself the WITI question (Why is this important?) can help you trace back to the fundamental goals, which may in turn help you identify whether the problem statement is properly framed.

Area 2: Consider Controllability

Before I delve into this section, I want to point out that people often use the term nudge very generally (by applying the term to all types of behavioral science interventions). That said, having more precise definitions and a taxonomy for different behavioral science interventions is useful to understanding deliberate, ethical design. Let's see how.

In the *Journal of Medical Ethics*, Yashir Saghai puts forth an excellent taxonomy that relates the degree to which influencers control influencees' behavior, the range of options made available to influencees, and the types of influence (Saghai 2013). To summarize and build on Saghai's thinking[19], examine controllability from a few perspectives:

1. **Look at things from the influencer side and consider where influence lands in the spectrum between fully controlling, substantially controlling, substantially non-controlling, or non-controlling behavior.** For example, eliminating choices from a set (e.g., a ban) might be considered fully controlling. On the other end of the spectrum, simply using forms of rational persuasion might be considered fully non-controlling. Somewhere in-between, an influencer might use incentives or disincentives.

2. **Look at things from the influencee side and consider to what extent influencees can resist the explicit or implicit direction of the influencer.** For example, can influencees easily change a default option set up by the influencer? Or do influencees have to go through a lot of steps to change the defaults set up? As an example of the latter, consider the case where a person needs to dig through cryptic menus and screens to change privacy settings and opt-out of advertising.

3. **Consider to what extent System 1 or System 2 thinking is involved.** Saghai's framework generally covers designs related to intuitive, fast thinking processes (i.e., System 1). However, as we'll see later, designs that engage slower, more reflective thinking processes (i.e., System 2), in

---

[19] Saghai essentially defines a nudge as a subset of behavioral science influences that is substantially non-controlling, utilizes shallow cognitive processes (e.g., System 1), and increases the probability of an influencee choosing a particular outcome (relative to a base case or control condition).

cases, may be viewed as less controlling or at least more acceptable.[20]

Again, let's consider the case of Facebook at the beginning of this chapter. Consider the following types of questions:

- By manipulating the number of positive versus negative items people saw in news feeds, Facebook was triggering System 1 processes. To what extent was Facebook influencing emotions? Controlling behavior?
- To what extent did Facebook allow people to opt-out of the research study?

Controllability is a critical dimension to examine, both in public policy and private sector situations. In the next section, we'll examine the influence types in greater detail.

Area 3: Analyze Influence Type and Outcomes

In the same paper discussed in the prior section, Yashir Saghai put forth a useful taxonomy of eight illustrative influences. Listed below, I organize Saghai's list roughly in terms of least to most controlling. I also add the notion of constructed preferences (which I described in the footnotes of

---

[20] On a related note to System 2 thinking, designers and influencers should be aware of the notion of constructed preferences, a view that for many decision-making situations people's preferences are neither uncovered nor revealed per se (as in a archeological dig) but instead built (i.e., constructed as with architecture). In other words, sometimes people just don't know what they want beforehand. They have to form their preferences, perhaps in a guided way. John Payne, James Bettman, and David Schkade outline considerations in their paper, "Measuring Constructed Preferences: Towards a Building Code" (Payne, Bettman and Schkade 1999). The notion of a building code for constructed preferences can become especially important when decision situations are either unfamiliar, complex, or infrequently experienced. As it turns out, the notion of constructed preferences was a key concept that John Payne contributed during the ideation process for development of the Retirement Goal Planning System application (described in Chapter 4).

the prior section). Here's a list of influence types:
1. **Rational Persuasion** – involves the presentation of reasons why an influencee should willingly take a particular action. An example might be offering workers a reason to vote for one paint versus another when choosing a new color for a room, and presenting these choices in random order to minimize biases associated with choice ordering.
2. **"Narrow" Nudge** – a non-controlling method that involves the preservation of the original choice set and triggers shallow (System 1) cognitive processes to increase particular outcomes. An example might be placing a professionally managed fund (provided that such a fund is in the best interests of most people) as the first item in a list of retirement product choices that a worker can select.
3. **Constructed Preferences**[21] – involves helping the influencee build a baseline or better understanding of their preferences. This strategy may be especially useful when people have infrequent experiences with the decisions at hand. One example in the healthcare space might be around counseling related to certain cancer treatment approaches.
4. **Incentive** – a method that involves monetary or non-monetary benefits to influence desired behavior. An example might be doubling frequent flyer miles for particular timeframes.
5. **Disincentive** – a method that involves raising the monetary or non-monetary costs to influence desired behavior. An example might be penalizing

---

[21] Depending on implementation, the application of constructed preferences designs may vary in level of control (e.g., if the constructed preferences design embeds rational persuasion or education techniques versus behavioral prods). For example, imagine a salesperson who sells exotic insurance that you are unfamiliar with (e.g., terrorist insurance) and plays up vivid fears during the sales process while you are constructing your preferences.

people for registering corporate filings late, or charging consumers extra for using a credit card.
6. **Behavioral Prod** – involves substantially controlling methods to influence outcomes, often by triggering shallow cognitive processes. For example, these methods may be typical in the processes that some marketing and sales organizations use within companies (e.g., making offers irresistible such as sumptuous ads for desserts).
7. **Coercion** – involves threats to result in specific behavior. For example, an online group may warn a company that they will engage in a smear campaign if the company does not change its business practices.
8. **Compulsion** – use of physical force (or a digital equivalent) to result in specific behavior. For example, a person might be required to visit a registration center or branch office.
9. **Choice Elimination** – involves removing possibilities from a choice set. For example, a facility may discontinue the sale of canned soda drinks and instead offer only juice and water.

Designers and influencers should think about influence types as a way to understand both mechanisms used and degree of control exercised. Sometimes there may be academic literature that can help to inform points of view on the effect sizes that may be encountered when implementing certain influence types. For example, suppose being first on a list of options elevates the selection of the first option by as much as 10% due to a primacy bias. Generally the more control involved, the more one wants to be certain that a deliberate decision is made regarding alignment with constituent goals.

To finish up this section, I again leave you to think about some questions regarding the case of Facebook as described earlier. What influence types were involved when Facebook provided some people with more positive news events in their feed versus others with more negative news events? Were these nudges? What was the relative size of the effect on behavior of participants? Was it small?

Area 4: Look at Trust

The Twitter account for the Misbehaving Blog quoted Richard Thaler as saying, "You shouldn't nudge if it's not something you'd be willing to talk about publicly" (Misbehaving Blog account on Twitter @MisbehavingBlog 2015). I see that as a good litmus test of sorts to guide design, especially, but not limited to, nudges (as narrowly defined by Saghai) in the public sector. I also see it extremely strong candidate as a litmus test for the private sector. However, I find it harder to prescribe my blanket morals for other companies given their diverse governance structures and business models; companies need to make their own choices.

I see at least two primary perspectives from which to look at trust: 1) the extent of goal alignment between the nudger and nudgee, and 2) ownership considerations, especially in terms of the psychological as opposed to legal aspect of ownership.

Sunstein nationally surveyed people to see what they thought about the ethics of thirty-four nudges (Sunstein 2015). For example, Sunstein asked people what they thought about:
- mandatory calorie labels
- government encouraged enrollment in pension plans
- mandatory automatic enrollment in green energy
- default last name change upon marriage to that of husband
- public education campaign on transgender
- default donations to the Red Cross
- default assumption of Christianity for census data.

What did Sunstein find?
1. Generally, there is widespread support for nudges.
2. Support for nudges diminishes under two conditions: 1) if people distrust the motivations of the choice architects (nudgers) and 2) when people fear that outcomes might inconsistent with values or interests (e.g., if inertia and inattention work against people).

3. There is mildly greater support[22] for Systems 2 versus Systems 1 nudges.
4. The assessment of the acceptability of nudges is greatly affected by political valence.
5. Transparency of nudges should not, in general, reduce the effectiveness of nudges.

While Sunstein's research focus is on public sector considerations, it seems reasonable to hypothesize that a number of these considerations would apply to the private sector. The big ones that stand out are the general, widespread support and the extent of goal and value alignment between nudger and nudgee. This reinforces my suggestion at the start of the Nudge Psyche checklist to allocate time to analyzing the goals of various constituents.

Let's again reconsider the case of Facebook. Recall Figure 5.1, which has the bottom-line title, "Facebook tends not to score well on trust measures." From that case, let's also reconsider a piece of what commenter Survivor wrote (bold added by me):

"…the thought that someone may have manipulated **my emotional state** sickens me. And, having lived with a sociopath for most of my adult life, your response to what really was a terrible decision that **violated your users most basic rights** mimics the behaviors of the monster with whom I used to live…"

Clearly a lot of complicated emotions gripped the individual when they wrote those comments. The piece that I want to draw attention to is the psychological ownership piece. Psychological ownership is a complex, but potentially powerful force at work when it comes to behavior, as endowed parties

---

[22] Readers should refer to the original paper for more precise details. In a nutshell however, use of the term mildly greater support refers to two threads of evidence: 1) greater preferences of individuals for System 2 nudges as inferred by increased probabilities of individuals selecting System 2 nudges compared to a control condition versus System 1 nudges compared to a control condition, and 2) stated preferences of individuals for System 2 nudges when they were asked to directly compare a variety of System 1 and 2 nudges.

tend to value something more than they would if they were a neutral party. Psychological ownership can apply to both physical things (e.g., houses, watches, coffee mugs) and intangibles (e.g., accrued Social Security benefits, personal data, happiness). Psychological ownership is a central concept in laboratory studies of markets where sellers have been given (i.e., endowed with) coffee mugs but are only willing to accept (WTA) sales prices that are nearly double what buyers are willing to pay (WTP) (Kahneman, Knetsch and Thaler 1991)[23], real-world research that potentially explains part of why people tend to claim Social Security benefits earlier than they should from an economic perspective[24], and the strong feelings of Survivor. Thus, people who implement nudges should think about the role that psychological ownership plays.

Think about the role psychological ownership plays when it comes to implementing nudges.

Figure 5.4: Coffee Mug from Thalerfest 2015

---

[23] To drive the point home, as illustrated with a very clever coffee mug design (Figure 5.4) given away at an event in honor of Richard Thaler, psychological ownership is significant with willingness to accept greater than willingness to pay (i.e., WTP < WTA).

[24] I credit my wife, Suzanne Shu (Professor at UCLA Anderson School of Management), for this research concept.

That said, an individual's feelings about psychological ownership may not always be clear cut. For example, setting aside legalities, consider how you feel about the following scenarios:

- An online retailer uses data it collects regarding your purchases to recommend related retail products you might like to purchase by displaying them on the computer screen.
- An online retailer uses data it collects regarding your purchases of clothing to recommend events that you should potentially attend in the area so that you can wear the clothes to the event.
- An online retailer uses data it collects regarding your purchases and determines that you might be at risk of depression and might be interested in online chat services with a health professional.
- An online retailer uses behavioral data it collects regarding one of your dependent's purchase patterns, determines that they might be at risk of depression, and sends you a text message of concern.
- An online retailer uses data it collects regarding your purchases and determines that you might be more impulsive or impatient than others, and as a result provides System 1 nudges that might increase the number of goods you purchase.
- An online retailer uses data it collects regarding your purchases and determines that you might be more impulsive or impatient than others, and as a result provides System 1 nudges that might help you with self-control.

Although I don't know what kind of thoughts were swirling through your head as you went through these scenarios, your feelings probably varied depending on your perspectives of privacy, ownership of data, social considerations, and whether data was going to be used for or against you. Ask yourself a few questions: How much would I be willing to accept to sell the right for the online retailer to approach me for each of the scenarios above for a year? How much would the online retailer be willing to pay for those rights to engage you in those ways for a year? To what extent would you trust an online retailer that engaged you in the ways above? What if the legal rights were in a grey area? To what extent would your trust level change?

In closing this section, nudgers need to look at the role of trust in terms of the past, present, and future. The topic of trust is more complex than what I've described here. However when it comes to nudge design, organizations should at least examine both goal alignment and psychological ownership.

Area 5: Consider the Role of Fairness

Imagine you are a capuchin monkey in a social sciences laboratory. You have a comfortable life in a small cage just adjacent to another capuchin monkey, a nice neighbor that you've known for awhile, since your days in Brazil. Both you and your neighbor are smart. In fact, you've each been trained to perform a simple task. You can take rocks that you are given one at a time and use these rocks to pay for food. You are an omnivore, you eat all types of food. In the laboratory, it is customary to receive in exchange for a rock either a piece of cucumber or a grape. You like to eat, so receiving either type of food is fine. You could eat pieces of cucumbers all day, as could your neighbor. But you really like the taste of grapes, as does your neighbor!

Feeding time comes around and the person who exchanges rocks is ready to dispense food to both you and your neighbor. You start first. You get a rock from a dispenser and you reach through the cage to hand the rock to the person. The person gives you a piece of cucumber. You eagerly eat the piece of cucumber and turn to the dispenser to get another rock. As you turn to get the next rock, you happen to see over your shoulder that you neighbor is exchanging a rock, and the person gives your neighbor a grape!

Now you are really excited. You quickly get the rock and turn back to the person. You hand over the rock and the person gives you...a piece of cucumber. How do you feel? What do you do? Maybe the person made a mistake?

You see your neighbor exchanging another rock in exchange for...a grape! You get excited again and go back to the dispenser for another rock. You give the rock to the person, and you receive...a piece of cucumber. Now how do you feel? Oh.

The scenario I've outlined is based on research by Sarah Brosnan and Frans de Waal (Brosnan and de Waal 2003) and in particular on a video presented by Frans de Waal that shows the reaction of a capuchin monkey that was put in the shoes you were just in (Unknown: Published by TVPUniversity 2012). You can view the video (entitled "Capuchin monkeys reject unequal pay") by visiting the Support Materials section at www.InsideNudging.com. No words could quite capture what that video of the capuchin monkey does in terms of depicting what unfairness feels like.

How might one analyze fairness? For this topic, I suggest looking at concepts from the area of organizational justice. Based on experimental research by Jason Colquitt, there are four factors that play a role relative to answering the question of "What is fair?" (Colquitt 2001). I paraphrase these four dimensions here:

1. **Procedural Justice** – A characterization of the fairness of the process being used, such as to what extent people can express their views and feelings during the process; view the process as applied consistently, free of bias, based on accurate info, and ethical; and can appeal outcomes.
2. **Distributive Justice** – A characterization of the fairness or allocation of outcomes relative to goals, such as to what extent people feel the outcomes reflect efforts, norms, results, and performance.
3. **Interpersonal Justice** – A characterization of authority figures that may enact the process relative to how fairly people are treated in terms of politeness, dignity, and respect (may include truthfulness).
4. **Informational Justice** – A characterization of authority figures and how fairly and adequately they exchange ideas with people, such as through candid communications, thorough and reasonable explanations of processes, timely updates, and tailored communications relative to individual

needs.

The capuchin monkey that received the cucumbers instead of yummy grapes was likely extremely unhappy with distributive justice and confused about procedural justice. Hence, the monkey threw a fit and rejected the cucumber multiple times when unfairness came into play. So when you examine your designs relative to fairness, consider using the four dimensions I describe above, especially the first two items in the list (which cover a lot of ground for many situations).

Area 6: Explore Acceptability

The last topic in the Nudge Psyche checklist, under Nudgee Attitudes, is whether the nudge sees the intervention as acceptable. The acceptability and perceived effectiveness of certain choice architecture scenarios is being explored by Suzanne Shu, H. Min Bang, and Elke Weber (Shu, Bang and Weber August 2015).

Below I'd like you to consider two scenarios regarding the use of smaller versus larger plates (which is a subset of scenarios used in their research). Since food served on smaller plates seems like more food (even if the amount of food is the same), people generally feel fuller faster when they eat on small plates. As a result, people tend stop eating sooner and eat less. Here are the two scenarios:

- Scenario 1: Imagine that you have paid to eat lunch at a **buffet restaurant**. The **buffet** has recently switched from larger plates and bowls to smaller ones in an attempt to encourage people to eat less.
- Scenario 2: Imagine that you have paid to eat lunch at a **government-run cafeteria**. The **cafeteria** has recently switched from larger plates and bowls to smaller ones in an attempt to encourage people to eat less.

How would you rate the acceptability of Scenario 1 on a scale of 1 (low acceptability) to 7 (high acceptability)? How about Scenario 2? What do you think the motivations of the buffet restaurant are? What do you think the motivations of the government-run cafeteria are?

As it turns out, Shu and her colleagues have found on a broader scale that while there may be tendencies, there is no simple rule of thumb for nudge acceptability as a function of the type of choice architect (e.g., company versus government) of a nudge. Rather it is important to examine the perceived motivations of the choice architect (as these effects may dominate the effects of the type of choice architect). Shu and colleagues observed higher acceptability for designs where perceived motivations were more about sustainability or health reasons as opposed to financial reasons that benefit the choice architect.

Now let's consider another scenario outlined in the same paper, this time regarding a potential ban on the sale of big sizes of sugary drinks:
1. How effective do you think this change would be on **you**?
2. How effective do you think this change would be on **others**?

As backdrop to this scenario, behavioral science research provides evidence that judgment differences between self versus others are significant in numerous situations. However, I'm not aware of another paper that relates self versus others to choice architecture effectiveness and acceptability. What Shu and colleagues observed by asking questions like these is that acceptability increases when there is higher perceived effectiveness of the choice architecture on both oneself and others. Moreover, their findings suggest that choice architectures are more acceptable when they are seen to have an even bigger influence on others than oneself.

They also examined a larger set of questions about the acceptability of nudges, particularly those associated with defaults, framing, and choice set restrictions (e.g., bans). To make a long story short, their findings suggest the following actions around increasing the acceptability of designs:
1. Use positive frames (when aligned with goals).
2. Demonstrate effectiveness (through experience, alternatively though hypothetical descriptions).
3. Highlight effectiveness for others (preferable) versus self.
4. Build trust through highlighting intentions (e.g., sustainability and health are better than financial reasons).

5. Consider social dominance orientation (SDO)[25] (which correlates with political affiliation).

Key Takeaways

- **Strive to make deliberate choices about designs through an ethical lens** – As a first step, think about two parts: nudge design and nudgee attitudes. I've offered the Nudge Psyche checklist which looks at nudge design through examining goals, controllability, and influence type. The Nudge Psyche checklist also covers nudgee attitudes in terms of trust, fairness, and acceptability.
- **Area 1: Examine constituent goals** – At minimum, think about individuals and the company. You may also bring other constituents into the analysis like partners, intermediates, or even competitors.
- **Area 2: Consider controllability** – Designs range from substantial non-control to fully controlling. The range of resistibility in terms of easy resistance to harder resistance should also be a point of consideration. Also make sure to think about whether System 1 or System 2 frameworks should be used.
- **Area 3: Analyze influence types and outcomes** – Generally speaking, designs are non-neutral (although between-subject designs might be randomized to minimize effects and biases). Designs work in different ways, and they have

---

[25] Social dominance orientation is a psychological measure that reflects a person's preference for inequality between social groups (e.g., to what extent does one prefer one's in-group to dominate an out-group) (Pratto, et al. 1994). Alternatively stated, to what extent does one prefer intergroup relationships to be equal versus hierarchical? In the Nudge Psyche framework, I alternatively suggest that dimensions from moral psychology and the application of Moral Foundations Theory to politics might be helpful (Haidt 2013).

different effect sizes on outcomes. Use a taxonomy of influence types as one way to assess where your design stands relative to others.

- **Area 4: Look at trust** – Find out whatever you can regarding brand reputation and trust relative to the past, present, and future. Then examine goal alignment and psychological ownership relative to the design you plan to implement as these often relate to trust.
- **Area 5: Consider the role of fairness** – At minimum think about procedural justice (e.g., process) and distributive justice (e.g., outcomes). Also consider interpersonal justice (e.g., authorities and process) and informational justice (e.g., authorities and communications).
- **Area 6: Explore acceptability** – Where possible with designs, use positive framing, demonstrate effectiveness (experienced or hypothetical), highlight effectiveness for others (preferable) versus self, highlight intentions such as sustainability or health to build trust, and consider social dominance orientation (which is an underlying driver correlated with political affiliation).

6
INSIDE RESEARCH AND TESTING

Take a moment to think about various sporting events you've seen broadcast on television, cable, or the Internet. Which sport do you think is the most boring to watch? Perhaps baseball? Or bowling? Or fishing? If you asked me in the mid-nineties what sport I thought was the most boring to watch, golf would have been up at the top of the list. Put me to sleep already. The interesting thing about golf is that it looks easy, but it is actually quite hard to do well. You have to understand core aspects like how the swing for the long game (where you hit the ball greater distances and seek rough placement of the ball) differs fundamentally from the swing for the short game (where precision is required to get the ball very close to or into the hole). You need to understand detailed physics and the interplay of equipment, such as the notion that when you want to hit the ball up into the air with an iron, you don't want to lift up on the swing or you may flub up the shot by topping the ball. Instead you want to hit the ball fairly level or even slightly downward to get the ball to go up because you rely on the angle of the club to lift the ball. And even after all of this, we haven't even scratched the surface on specialty situations, strategy, and the mindset of golf play. If you are a golfer, you might remember hitting that first ball where all of the complex stuff came together – the perfect shot that hooked you forever. For me, it was an iron shot off the tee at the 7th hole at the South Shore Golf Course in Chicago that stopped close to a foot from the hole.

My experience at Allianz Global Investors Center for Behavioral Finance was my 7th hole, iron shot in the field of behavioral science. It all came together for me in terms of connecting the dots between business strategy, detailed tactics, and doing good. I got hooked, especially with our work on PlanSuccess as described in Chapter 2. During my tenure consulting with Allianz Global Investors, and also with a number of other clients, I further developed an appreciation for research and testing. These are important topics for implementing behavioral science initiatives. Like golf, these topics look easy, but they are actually quite challenging to do well.

In this chapter, I'd like to cover three perspectives relative to research and testing challenges, and share some thoughts on what might be done to address these challenges. These perspectives are covered in three subsections:

- **Managing corporate-academic tension** - This subsection covers tension stemming from different roles and backgrounds.
- **Mining research and handling the field** - This subsection covers gaps related to connecting research with the real world.
- **Testing travails** - This subsection covers common situations where many companies can simply do better.

Managing Corporate-Academic Tension

Research can be viewed as an investment that involves risk. That is, we often don't know to what extent research will yield successful outcomes or not. So it is instructive to take a closer look at how people make decisions involving risk. Consider the following example posed by Amos Tversky and Daniel Kahneman (Tversky and Kahneman 1981) and identify what you would choose:

Imagine that you face the following pair of concurrent decisions. First examine both decisions, then indicate the options you prefer.
Decision (i). Choose between:
A. a sure gain of $240
B . 25% chance to gain $1000, and 75% chance to gain nothing
Decision (ii). Choose between:
C. a sure loss of $750
D. 75% chance to lose $1000, and 25% chance to lose nothing

Which options did you choose? If you are like most people in Tversky and Kahneman's study, then you chose option A for the first decision (84 percent of people) and option D for the second decision (87 percent of people).

There are two interesting observations about these decisions:

- **Observation 1: People tend to make risk averse choices when faced with gains.** In the first decision, people tend to seek a certain win of $240 as opposed to a risky outcome of winning either $1000 or $0. In other words, when facing gains, we tend to go for the certain choice (i.e., no risk).
- **Observation 2: People tend to be make risk seeking choices when faced with losses.** In the second decision, rather than face a certain loss of $750, people tend to seek a risky outcome of losing either $1000 (more money) or $0. In other words, when facing losses, we tend to go for the risky choice (the gamble).[26]

Yet think about the following example (Tversky and

---

[26] I've always remembered how loss aversion affects decision making by thinking about the story of a person who owes the Mafia a significant amount of money and fears the certainty of repercussions (e.g., physical losses or death). As such, in an effort to try to get themselves out of the hole the person decides to double-up their risk and goes to the casino to gamble. The consequences are that they may dig themselves an even bigger hole. While this story is more about decisions in the face of catastrophic losses, I still find that the story helps people remember how loss aversion affects decisions.

Kahneman 1981).
Choose between:
A & D. 25% chance to win $240, and 75% chance to lose $760.
B & C. 25% chance to win $250, and 75% chance to lose $750.

Which options did you choose now? If you are like most people in Tversky and Kahneman's study, then you chose B & C (100 percent of people) because the outcomes are better than the A & D choice for every outcome. But did you notice that the choices in this latter example are simply a combination of the choices in the prior example? If that is the case, then why do people tend to switch from choosing A & D in the first example to B & C in the second example? The reason is that people tend to look at the decisions in the first example in isolation as opposed to as a portfolio of decisions. So isolated choices can lead to suboptimal choices, which leads to the next observation.

Observation 3: People often think too narrowly, such as overlooking the role of portfolios. It is important to remember that investments should not be looked at in isolation. For example, on its own an investment in homeowner's insurance looks terrible; the investment has a negative expected return. However, the investment in insurance for a house can make sense if one actually owns the house being insured. If the house doesn't burn down, then one still has a house and paid out premiums for insurance. If the house burns down, then one has lost the house but will be receive money in compensation for the loss. The value of an investment depends on the portfolio of the holder. While the concept of a investment portfolio is a core idea in finance, these management principles often get overlooked when corporations start to think about investments in behavioral science research.

These thoughts on risk and portfolios, which only scratch the surface on the research on those topics, are relevant for understanding how to approach the risks inherent in research and testing. To further understand those risks, here are some paraphrased statements that also reflect the tension between the corporate and academic worlds related to research and testing:

- Corporate practice leader: "Why do we need research and testing? Can't we just directly leverage results from the academic papers?"
- Academic: "We'll need to manage expectations with management about this study. I don't think they realize that less than 30% of studies yield positive results."
- Corporate product manager: "We do a lot testing on our website to determine how to get the best results."
- Behavioral scientist: "The company does a lot of testing, but I'm not sure any of the results can be trusted. A lot of the studies are confounded. It seems the company just wants to throw everything in but the kitchen sink to try to get results. For the future, it's important that we design tests properly, isolate the various effects, and be certain to test one thing at a time. Otherwise, we won't really know what conclusions to draw from our studies."
- Corporate program manager: "The academics have introduced some really cool, innovative ideas. But they do not seem to understand that building the underlying research and testing capability would take significant effort."
- Academic: "The company thinks we're prophets, and we do know lots of things, but the field of behavioral science has many unknowns. Many things need to be tested because we simply do not know the answers. Innovating and doing the job right take time."

What can be done to manage corporate-academic tension? Here are some things to think about:

1. **Clarify the strategic goals and model relative to integrating behavioral science into the organization.** For example, to what extent is the strategy around thought leadership? Product development and innovation? Optimization of the existing business? By discussing strategy, parties can better align on the spectrum of potential

outcomes and risks.
2. **Develop a framework for thinking about risk, managing risk, and openly talking about it.** This includes looking at individual projects and risk relative to investment amounts, potential upsides and downsides, and probabilities of outcomes. But it also involves thinking about the portfolio of projects being pursued. For example, it may be desirable to have a blend of projects that include quick-win types with lower risk and longer-term types with higher risk and potentially higher payoff outcomes.
3. **Recognize that doing good work takes effort, time, and investment.** Most of the companies that I've worked with tend to move too fast and err on the side of cutting too many corners on either background research, the required participants needed for a test, the research design, or on the development of a testing environment. Now to be fair, my observation is relative to what I see in the academic community and peer-reviewed scientific journals, where control and rigor are required. While I totally appreciate the desire for companies to move fast, I do think there is a tendency to underestimate the effort required to do things properly. Companies need to develop a better appreciation for scientific approaches. Academics need to improve their awareness of corporate constraints.

Mining Research and Handling the Field

Research papers, specifically papers published in academic journals, form the foundation for the body of existing behavioral science research. The types of papers vary widely. To provide some sense of variety, some papers survey and summarize a broad landscape of research papers. Others involve looking at existing data in the market (e.g., such as asset prices) and try to explain different phenomena (e.g., such as implied equity premiums in the financial markets). Some papers may include simulations based on both existing and posited theoretical models. Yet other studies involve laboratory or survey work where study participants are recruited, randomly assigned to treatment groups, and provided with varying stimuli to see how they behave relative to the stimuli. There are also field studies, which attempt to go into the real world and see how people behave. Then there are quantitative studies of studies, known as meta studies, which may try to look at research papers with a common theme and try to distill and quantify the effect sizes and findings across the set of studies under examination.

I find that business people often underestimate what it takes to do good scientific work, and I thought it would be useful to shed some light on this. In my research, I found two business school-centric articles that collectively estimate the average cost of an academic research paper published in a top-tier journal to be between $400,000 per paper (Terwiesch and Ulrich 2014) and $1,500,000 per *actionable* paper (Martin 2012).[27] Very loosely speaking, the term actionable refers to research that is usable by business managers (versus by only other academics, say). More precise definitions of actionable research and measurements are outlined by Jone Pearce and Laura Huang in their research (Pearce and Huang 2012).

While the structure and approach of behavioral science research papers vary, I want to provide additional detail on one frequently encountered structure. Shedding light on the structure of research papers can help provide insights as to why valuable gems can be mined from these papers. As an example, let's look at the paper, "Life expectancy as a constructed belief: Evidence of a live-to or die-by framing effect" (Payne, Sagara, et al. 2013). Key elements of this paper include:

1. **Abstract and Background** - Research papers commonly include a summary of headline findings along with some context as to what extent the

---

[27] To provide additional color, Roger Martin estimates the number of actionable papers in top-tier journals to make up roughly one-third of total research paper production output in the business academic world, whereas non-actionable papers make up roughly two-thirds of the total.

research is applicable for other research, social, or business issues. In the paper by Payne and colleagues:

- A headline finding is that when people estimate how long they will live, irrelevant factors such as how a question is asked or framed can significantly influence estimates. For example, some people were asked to estimate the probability of living to a particular age (say a specific age milestone such as 65, 75, 85, or 95). Others were asked about the probability of dying by that same age or younger. In theory, these numbers should add up to 100 percent if everyone calculated probabilities like economists and were insensitive to framing effects. That is, the live-to age should be the same as die-by age. However, people were very sensitive to framing effects. When plotting estimates of probabilities of living against age, longevity estimates by those in the live-to frame were 7.38 to 9.17 years longer than the die-by frame.
- The paper also provides background on why research in this area is important. For example, some 80 million baby boomers have to plan for uncertain and potentially long periods of retirement. Boomers may have to plan for situations where they live ten, twenty, or even more than thirty years past the age of retirement. The process of estimating (or at least thinking about) longevity is important.

2. **Prior Research** - Research papers generally also provide citations to other research that serve as a context for the current research. For example, there may be citations to foundational research, related research, and other research using different approaches. These citations can be useful for

scholars and sometimes useful for practitioners. In the example paper we are looking at:
- The authors shed light on other life expectation surveys, such as that done with the Health and Retirement Study (HRS) since the early nineties or studies sponsored by the Federal Reserve.
- There are also citations to other nuggets of research which may provide insights on special conditions related to the area of study. For example, the authors relate a publication covering evidence that teenagers are pessimistic relative to life expectations and that pessimistic outlooks may be due to perceived lack of control during that phase of life (Fischhoff, et al. 2000).

3. **Studies Examining Basic Effect** - A common element to many behavioral science research papers is the inclusion of one or more studies. Studies may involve A/B testing (as first described in Chapter 4) and randomizing the assignment of participants to different conditions and seeing whether outcomes are different between the conditions. Again, in the paper we are examining by Payne and colleagues:
- In the first study of the paper, the researchers gathered a wide range of people ages 18 to 83 years of age with half of the respondents (call them being assigned to the "A" or "live-to" condition) being asked to provide probabilities of living to a certain age or older and the other half (call them being assigned to the "B" or "die-by" condition) being asked about dying by a certain age or younger. As mentioned previously, the largest effect included a difference of 9.17 years being added to the mean life expectancy predictions when people were in the live-

to condition.
- In the second study of the paper, the researchers narrowed the demographics to focus on those from 45 to 65 years old (Note that these are people that are closer to having to think about retirement issues in some sense). They also collected information on self-reported health status to analyze the relationship with life expectancy predictions. In this second study they found a difference of 7.38 years being added to the mean life expectancy predictions when people were in the live-to condition.

4. **Study Examining Broader Behavioral Science** - In addition to addressing various stimuli presented to participants and characterizing resulting effect sizes, research papers may also focus on studying the underlying psychology more closely. The paper by Payne and colleagues also tries to do this through adding a third study:
    - In this study within the paper, the researchers examine the underlying cognitive processes that people use by seeing to what extent the types of information people retrieve from thinking affect their predicted probability of being alive at the age of 85. They do this by first asking people to report any thoughts that they had in their minds as they consider the possibility of living-to or dying-by a certain age (again people are randomly assigned to live-to or die-by conditions), having people report their probability of living-to or dying-by a certain age, and then coding their pre-reported thoughts (e.g., classifying each thought as more about living, dying, or neither).
    - The researchers essentially find (through a statistical technique known as mediation

analysis) that people had more positive thoughts in the live-to condition which in turn increases their predicted probability of being alive at the age of 85. In summary, this third study goes deeper and essentially provides further evidence about how people construct their beliefs about longevity (e.g., retrieving more positive thoughts tends to increase the predicted probability of living).

5. **Implications** – Research papers also commonly include an implications section which may address other researchers, specific uses in the industry, or both. In my view, research tends to be more actionable when it includes both 1) conceptual knowledge that can be generalized to other situations and 2) concrete implications or applications outside of the laboratory and in the real world. With respect to the Payne et al. paper they relate the research to an important (and often undervalued) product class in the financial services and insurance space:

- The researchers covered a study that relates a person's beliefs about their own life expectancy to a purchase probability of an insurance product known as a life annuity, a product which essentially provides the insured a certain degree of financial safety from the risks of living a long time. The hypothetical life annuity in this particular study guaranteed an amount of money the insured would receive every year as long as they live, starting at 65 years old.
- They found that the likelihood of people who wanted to purchase the annuity was 39 percent for those who judged themselves to live longer versus 26 percent who judged themselves less likely to live longer and that the effect was strongest for

those in the live-to frame.

Let's take a step back as to why I wanted to describe what a behavioral science research paper looks like along with some example findings:
- The papers are often misunderstood and may not even be read by many business people.
- There are hidden gems in these papers and opportunities to mine them.
- Gems in these papers can include headline findings, subfindings, effect sizes, nuances, other relevant background material, insights, and seeds for inspiration.

Yet there are some clear caveats for mining this type of research:
- It takes a skilled resource to mine this type of material. It suggests thinking about the company's research operations and support model.
- There are nuances associated with distinguishing between research in a core science area (such as general judgment and decision making research) versus research specific to an industry and domain (such as research related the effectiveness of financial advisors) and applying the research appropriately.
- Many of the studies in research papers occur in controlled environments. Related to this are considerations about replicating effects in the real world and predicting whether effect sizes would likely decrease or increase when brought into the real world. (Note that interested parties could either investigate meta studies that might have been done and compare lab versus the field or seek advice and perspectives from behavioral scientists.)

As I've mentioned before, research is an important part of the GRIT™ framework. So let me wrap up this section on mining research and handling the field by offering some things to think about:

1. **Research can provide some real gems, so think about and develop a research strategy.** Does it make sense to at least try to leverage existing research? Can we benefit either as a thought leader or improve our operations by pursuing field research? What possibilities might exist if we try to integrate behavioral science research into our product innovation processes?
2. **Mining research and performing research can be somewhat challenging, so think about the operations and support model.** In Appendix A, I identify some potential elements to consider as a company starts to operationalize behavioral science. For example, a company might benefit by hiring or contracting out resources related to science officer, advisory board, researchers, and academic partnerships.
3. **Stretch your thinking a look for creative opportunities to leverage behavioral science as a company energizer.** Perhaps consider customer advisor board opportunities as a way to get closer to customers. Perhaps establish lighthouse account relationships where early adopters get additional benefits and have substantial branding to attract other customers. See how thought leadership can play a role relative to branding, marketing, and business development. Seek out partners that can apply behavioral science and help with product development and innovation ideas.

Testing Travails

Consider the following setting. A company and an academic advisory group get together to do research testing. They dive into running different testing scenarios, and the two parties struggle coming from different perspectives as to what constitutes controlled testing and what constitutes success. The company believes in getting results. The academic advisory group believes in careful control. As the parties struggle, each party transforms through the process. What will happen with the individual testing scenarios? How will the overall collaboration and story turn out?

Let's go further and suppose that the company is an life annuity provider that is trying to explore testing directly related to the laboratory research on live-to and die-by framing as outlined by Payne and colleagues in the prior section (Payne, Sagara, et al. 2013). For example, suppose the company wanted to implement a version of the questionnaire for part of their website experience before people express their expectations on longevity:

1. **Why might the company want to test?** On one end of the spectrum they might simply want to test to see if the functionality works. Or they might want to see if people get confused by the questionnaire or drop out early in the process. On the other end of the spectrum, they might want to see if one way of framing the question (say the live-to condition) generates either longer estimates of longevity or more accurate estimates relative to actuarial tables. The company might want to test because they either want to maximize profits of their insurance products (within legal constraints) or strike the right balance in helping the individual find the right product. The company should look at their goals as per the Behavioral GRIT™ model.

2. **What should the company test?** There are a lot of considerations to think about, and I'll just scratch the surface here and describe some very top-level testing concepts. These concepts are core to the academic world but frequently less understood in the business world. These points are related to a concept known as the *research design* (or *experimental design*). What follows are some example scenarios which shed some light on top-level considerations regarding the research design:

    - In the example we are using, if the company wanted to test the live-to and die-by concept outside of the lab and on an actual website in the field, the most consistent way to implement the research design (relative to the original research) would be to randomly assign users as they arrive on the website to either the live-to or die-by group conditions and then analyze differences between the two groups. This research design would be known as a *between-subject* research design.

- Suppose that the website instead asked users two questions: the first asking them what age they thought they would live to, and the second asking them what age they thought they would die by? Setting aside the complications associated with sequencing effects (like potential biases introduced by the order of the questions, such as being anchored by the answer to the first question), such an approach would be called a *within-subject* research design.

- Yet as another case, suppose that for the first week the company asked users visiting the website the live-to questions. Then the second week, the company asked users visiting the website the die-by questions. This structure would be a *time-based, before-and-after* research design. Other issues can arise with this type of approach. For example, imagine a negative, world health event occurs during the second week of the test. The occurrence of this event might negatively bias the answers of users in the second group.

- The point of this discussion has been to shed some light on high-level research design considerations that need to be addressed. And while there may be a preference for a particular research design from scientific perspective, there may be other considerations such as technical difficulties of implementation, budgets, tactical issues, and legal considerations that might put constraints on what can be executed.

3. **How should the company test?** As a company starts to think more deeply about how testing will be done, there will be more detailed considerations to work through. Example considerations include:

- **Participants** - What will be the target profile or segment for participants? Will they be acquired in a lab environment or in the field?
- **Research Design** - This is the definition and soup-to-nuts recipe for the testing study. If the study will be outsourced or constructed in-house, there should be clear requirements specification for this.
- **Development** - Studies may require programming for a lab environment (such as on a software platform like Qualtrics) or a production environment (like a company's proprietary software platform). Will the company use internal or external resources?
- **Data Analysis** - Once data has been collected, to what extent has the company thought about how analysis of the data will be done? What statistical approaches might be used, and does the company have the right resources?
- **Performance Measurements** – It is often desirable to have very clear performance measures. In fact, research designs may not even be able to be done properly without specifying the goals and measures. For example, should conditions within the research design try to increase sales leads? Feelings of fairness by customers? Maximize sales for a particular product?

I started this section with the setting of an academic advisory group and a company collaborating on testing. What are some examples of where tensions or problems arise?

- **Goal and process alignment issues** - The company wants to throw the kitchen sink at improving the bottom line, and the academic participants would like to proceed systematically and explore intellectually interesting work. Proceeding quickly can yield good outcomes if one is lucky. But proceeding too quickly can backfire; things can be missed. It should also be recognized that the motivations of academic participants also needs to be matched with the needs of the company. For example, some academics may only participate in research to the extent that it can help them with developing work that can be published in a scientific journal.

- **Research design and execution issues** – While some companies seem to ignore A/B testing, others run a lot of tests. But in the tests I've seen companies create, two issues or concerns come up repeatedly during scientific reviews: 1) research design issues such as changing too many things between the A and B groups so that the contributing factors are confounded and effects cannot be isolated[28] and 2) selection bias when

---

[28] In some cases we have offered guidelines to companies when constructing tests so that they can better isolate the contributing factors. Three frequent guidelines include addressing notions of 1) attribution, 2) substitutability, and 3) affect. Attribution refers to adding one thing to the base case. Substitutability refers to replacing something. So as an example regarding attribution, suppose condition A involves exercise once per week but no medicine. Then condition B might involve exercise once per week and the addition of a daily pill containing medicine. As an example regarding substitutability, suppose in condition A the web pages include pricing information in stated in monthly amounts. In condition B, the pricing information might substituted with annual amounts. The idea of affect is that someone should be able to look at certain critical information and have an immediate feeling of

assigning participants to the A and B groups.
- **Lack of a testing platform approach** - Many companies have a one-off approach to testing. Creating a single test study becomes a monumental hurdle when the company has not invested in the discipline to create a testing and learning culture.
- **Lack of deliberate ethical considerations for critical areas** - While most research and design work does not blow up or harm participants, recall some of the cases I portrayed in Chapter 5. It is possible that some of the studies would have had better outcomes if the testing design had been more deliberately considered by executive management or run through an independent review board (if not by a university review board then perhaps by a third-party review board like IntegReview at www.integreview.com).

Testing is an important part of the GRIT™ framework. There are two sources that I would recommend for readers to explore things further. The first is a book by Dilip Soman, called *The Last Mile* (Soman 2015). Whereas this book is more focused on the management aspects of behavioral science initiatives, Soman's book goes in to practitioner-level detail on applying specific behavioral science concepts. He also has a very good chapter specifically on experiments and trials. The other book I recommend is *Inside the Nudge Unit* by David Halpern (Halpern 2015). Halpern's book provides some excellent examples of real field tests and randomized control trials in the public sector, and he also presents some high-level results. In any case, let me wrap up this section and offer some

---

whether something is good or bad. For example, highlighting to a consumer projected savings of $100 off a product without additional context might lack affect. The person might be wondering whether the retail price of the product is $400 or $3,000. However, if a consumer is provided information that the retail price is normally $400, then they will more likely have an immediate feeling as to whether the amount of savings is good (or bad), in this case because they have a reference point.

things to think about:
1. **Develop a testing strategy** - Consider what the goals of testing should be. For example, do goals include influencing outcomes? In what way? Is testing about risk management? Is testing about filtering out ideas or testing the viability of really new ideas? If so, how rapidly does the company want to learn? To what extent can the company develop a pipeline of tests, a prioritization framework for the individual tests, and key champions for the tests? To what extent does the company want to invite customers into the testing process?
2. **Develop a testing platform** - When I refer to a testing platform, it means to develop capabilities to do regular testing (of multiple types) and go beyond one-off tests. While some companies do not perform any quantitative testing whatsoever, some companies look at testing in a production environment where consumers form actual preferences and make choices. These companies may then have analytical techniques for mining the data and seeing how outcomes were influenced. Going beyond production environment testing into a laboratory environment setup might additionally help to open up other possibilities. For example, in a laboratory environment a company might be able to use eye tracking technology to see where consumers actually look (which provides more insight about their intermediate behavior and thinking) versus where they move their cursor or click (which mostly just captures the end decision) during a customer experience.[29] Or in a lab environment a company might be able to test the impact of different website layouts.[30] A lab can

---

[29] See the Support Materials section for this book at www.InsideNudging.com for an example of eye tracking technology.
[30] There are a number of software companies that provide

help a company filter out undesirable or unsuccessful concepts before taking them to production environments. Finally, a lab might also help to remove political constraints from the design process and allow a company to develop much wilder ideas that lead to success.

3. **Refine research design and testing execution capabilities** – I suggest companies develop a respect and discipline for testing from design through test execution and analysis. Some companies would do well by establishing a behavioral science officer role and getting research support resources to help get this type of discipline started properly. Other possibilities include bringing in someone to coach personnel on proper research design and analysis, say on a one-time or regular basis. In order to integrate the learning process into the business, companies may wish to set up sessions to review actual, planned tests with specialized or academic advisors contracted outside the company. Finally, developing testing discipline means actively thinking through things. Below is a checklist that I've sometimes provided to client companies so that they can better help themselves when it comes to developing testing discipline.

Behavioral Science Thinking Checklist
a. Purpose of the test (and some details about what we hope to learn)
b. Hypothesis
   i. What matters
   ii. Why we think it matters (and why we think the hypothesis is true)
   iii. Any assumptions

---

testing tools of this nature that can be used on websites in production environments (and diminish the desirability of a separate testing environment). However, there may be software development, integration, or security issues that still make establishing a testing environment very desirable.

      c. Description of the design
          i. Any assumptions about design
          ii. Description of the overall structure of the total conditions (e.g., A/B, 3x2 dimensional) and of each condition being tested (plus which variable is being manipulated in each condition)
          iii. Description of participant pool
              1. Source, demographics, etc.
              2. How we will minimize selection bias
              3. Number of participants powering the study (and how power was estimated or validated)
      d. Other details of the test
          i. Timing
          ii. Differences between test and production environments
          iii. Analysis approach
          iv. Performance measurement
          v. Other
      e. Business requirements
          i. Strategy options and selection
          ii. Customers and tactics
          iii. Consent
          iv. Independent review board
          v. Other

Key Takeaways

The purpose of this chapter was to shed light on management issues related to managing research and testing issues associated with behavioral science initiatives. I examined three angles:

- **Managing corporate-academic tension** – Here I suggested that companies really spend time to think about strategic goals and the integration model for behavioral science. I also encouraged a framework for openly discussing and managing risk, as research and testing are inherently uncertain activities. Finally, I encouraged companies to set the proper expectations that good research takes time.

- **Mining research and handling the field** – In this subsection, I provided a manager's introduction to what scientific research papers look like. I highlighted that there are some real gems within the existing body of scientific research, but I also highlighted unknowns and the need for companies to figure out how they will mine research. I also suggested that companies can also look to behavioral science as a company energizer through changing the customer relationship or feeding the innovation process.

- **Testing travails** - In this subsection, I highlighted some things that can go wrong with the testing activities by a company, such as goal and process alignment, research design and execution issues, one-off approaches, and deliberate ethical considerations. I encouraged companies to think about their testing strategy, develop a testing platform, and develop a discipline around testing. I offered a behavioral science thinking checklist as a possible tool for starting down the path of better testing.

7
NUDGING TO DEMOCRATIZE OUTCOMES

Since the first edition of *Inside Nudging*, I've had the opportunity to work on some interesting projects and research which aligns with my personal goals to do more good for the world. I wanted to share a few of those experiences with you in hope that it might give you some ideas about how to nudge for good and democratize outcomes.

Individual Behavioral Differences

In Chapter 1, I intimated that a significant proportion of the implementations of choice architecture in the real world uses a mass, one-size-fits-all approach. That is, such approaches try to maximize outcomes through implementing a single, "best" environment for the entire target audience. There's little to no variation in the choice environment based on particular needs of the individual. While such an approach may have strengths in terms of simplicity, it may fall short in terms of addressing certain people based on their individual behavioral differences.

What are individual behavioral differences? While many companies use demographic differences to analyze and target populations, such as by gender, age, household income, and educational level, individual behavioral differences relate to various psychological, judgment, and belief-driven differences in how people make decisions.

As an example of individual behavioral differences, consider the following chart (Figure 7.1), which is based on a survey I worked on with Kendra Seaman, Mikella Green, and Gregory Samanez-Larkin and covers 508 healthy people between the ages of 20 and 81 (Seaman, Green, et al. 2018). The chart illustrates the distribution of survey participants' loss aversion scores[31], which are essentially their sensitivity to losses relative to gains. In this sample, the median loss aversion score was about 1.75 (i.e., such people experience losses 1.75 times as intensely as gains). Yet on the right hand side of the chart, 10.8% of people had loss aversion scores greater than 9.0 and less than or equal to 10.0. That is pretty extreme sensitivity to losses. At the other end of the spectrum on the left hand side of the chart, 18.9% of people (i.e., 13.8% plus 5.1%) were either 1) just as sensitive to losses as gains or 2) somewhat gain seeking. People may make very different decisions according to their loss aversion sensitivities, and these differences extend to many other behavioral areas beyond those covered here.

Why do individual differences matter? Whereas demographic information may factually represent *what* you are, individual behavioral differences speak more to *who* you are and how you perceive the world and behave. Think about the case of loss aversion for a moment. If someone is extremely loss averse, how should they think about financial decisions? Should they invest significant amounts of money in risky stocks if they need that money? Should they take on adjustable rate mortgages? How should they look at insurance? While the answers are not necessarily clear cut, by looking at people through the lenses of individual behavioral differences, we can better understand how choice environments might differentially affect people or be tailored to help meet their needs.

---

[31] You can measure your own loss aversion score for free by visiting the Digitai website: http://www.digitai.org/#lab

Example of Individual Behavioral Differences: Percent of People and Their Loss Aversion

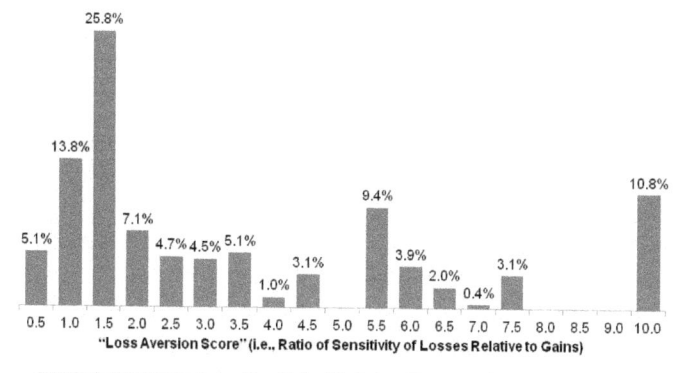

- 0.5: 5.1%
- 1.0: 13.8%
- 1.5: 25.8%
- 2.0: 7.1%
- 2.5: 4.7%
- 3.0: 4.5%
- 3.5: 5.1%
- 4.0: 3.1%
- 4.5: 1.0%
- 5.0: 9.4%
- 5.5: 3.9%
- 6.0: 2.0%
- 6.5: 0.4%
- 7.0: 3.1%
- 10.0: 10.8%

"Loss Aversion Score" (i.e., Ratio of Sensitivity of Losses Relative to Gains)

Source: Based on data from Seaman, Kendra and Green, Mikella and Shu, Stephen and Samanez-Larkin, Gregory. (2018). Individual Differences in Loss Aversion and Preferences for Skewed Risks Across Adulthood. *Psychology and Aging*, 33(4), 654.

Copyright © 2019 by Steve Shu Consulting

Figure 7.1: Example Distribution of Loss Aversion Scores, an Individual Behavioral Difference

Let's examine another individual behavioral difference, specifically around subjective numeracy. Consider the following questions, where answers to each question are supposed to be an integer between 1 and 6 (McNaughton, Cavanaugh, et al. 2015):

1) How good are you at working with fractions? (1 = not good at all and 6 = extremely good)

2) How good are you at figuring out how much a shirt will cost if it is 25% off? (1 = not good at all and 6 = extremely good)

3) How often do you find numerical information to be useful? (1 = never and 6 = very often).

The answers to these questions (called "items"), when summed together, result in a number between 3 and 18 called a scale.[32] In this case, the sum of the three numbers results in a

---

[32] In the interest of brevity, I do not define how scales are

measure of subjective numeracy, which represents a combination of 1) a person's self-reported skills relative to handling numbers and math related to percentages, etc. and 2) their information preferences. For example, a person who has a subjective numeracy score of 3 could be considered much less numerate than a person with a score of 18. People with a score of 3 might be intimidated by using percentages either because they do not feel they have the skill to compute the answers or because they fail to find numerical information useful. Now suppose these same people are asked whether they wish to save 3% of their salary. Might they have difficulty? Might they be discriminated against because they are less numerate? Evidence suggests that they might be.

In 2018 I started to run a series of lab studies[33] which framed retirement savings decisions in terms of "pennies per dollar of salary" instead of "percent of salary".[34] I analyzed the psychology going on in people's minds and their choices. Furthermore, I used both a mixture of subjective numeracy and financial literacy scales to assess the differential impacts of the information architecture on people's judgments and decisions. To make a long story short, the study results indicate that pennies reframing could result in the average person making choices which would lead to on the order of 20% more savings in retirement (in comparison to the current practice of using percent of salary framing). But more importantly, pennies reframing could result in 60% more savings for lower income people (say earning $25,000 per year) who are the least financially literate. While it has yet to be seen to what extent these results will extend from the lab to the real world (I am in the process of seeking a field host at the time of this writing),

---

constructed and tested. Suffice it to say, scales should be valid (i.e., actually measure what we intend to measure) and reliable (i.e., measure things consistently).
[33] Shu, Stephen. "Pennies Reframing and Savings." Working paper, 2019.
[34] The origins of the "pennies" concept comes from a very seasoned financial advisor and friend of mine, George Fraser. George owns a Pennies on the Dollar trademark as part of GKCPV Investments.

even if they do so only to a small extent, it will be an important step toward democratizing retirement savings outcomes.

The Digital World

The digital world offers a number of opportunities to democratize outcomes. Companies that have put modern technology infrastructure and operational processes in place can better capitalize on agility and scale than those companies that have not. Most importantly, agile companies can in theory deploy value more quickly as supported by A/B testing platform capabilities (such as mentioned in Chapter 6).

At the same time, the digital world brings great responsibility. On the one hand, we have evidence that people behave differently using digital devices, in domains such as comprehension, visual biases (e.g., edge aversion), and a number of other areas (Benartzi and Lehrer 2017). On the other hand, technology has become increasingly complicated with large teams required to develop, test, and maintain technology infrastructure. Have these companies put the right processes in place to address behavioral science considerations, including new findings in the digital age? And if they have put processes in place, are they of the right scale? My anecdotal experience indicates that these two conditions may not be satisfied in many companies. For example, I often see critical aspects of choice architecture inadvertently left to technology developers who may neither have behavioral science nor design on their list of concerns for a variety of reasons.

The digital world brings scale in terms of reaching end users, and if we are smart, we can use this scale to improve outcomes and reduce discrimination. Hal Hershfield, Shlomo Benartzi, and I ran a study with the FinTech company Acorns, a business which made its name early on through the concept of investing "spare change" (Hershfield, Shu & Benartzi 2019). For example, suppose a user of the Acorns app bought a cup of coffee for $4.25. The app would allow the user to round up the purchase to $5.00 with $0.75 being moved into an account that allowed micro-amounts to be invested in portfolios with various risk/return profiles.

In the study we ran, our goal was to go beyond purchase-associated savings and instead increase the percentage of savers saving regularly through participation in a recurring deposit program. For a subset of new users to the app, we presented them with an opportunity to join this recurring savings program with 1) some of the people being offered the option to save $150 per month, 2) some of the people being offered the option to save $35 per week, and 3) some of the people being offered the option to save $5 per day. So people in each of these three groups were offered choices that were roughly equivalent in terms of economic consequences, but the choices were presented in a different way for each group.

How did people behave, and what were their choices? Whereas 7.1% of people joined the recurring deposit program when it was framed as $150 per month, 10.3% of people joined when it was framed as $35 per week. And a whopping 29.9% of people joined when it was framed as $5 per day. Whether more people joined because they experienced less psychological pain, thought of opportunity costs differently through the framing, or some other reason, the end result was that four times as many users joined the program when it was framed as $5 per day instead of $150 per month.

When examining the results of the study more closely, we also find interesting results relative to the impact on different income levels. While on average 7.1% of people had signed up for the recurring deposit program when it was framed as $150 per month, that average sign-up rate actually reflects 15% of people signing up who earn more than $100,000 per year and only 5% of people signing up who earn less than $25,000 per year (See the left side of Figure 7.2). In other words, there is a sign-up impact of three times the amount for higher versus lower income levels. However, when the recurring deposit program was framed as $5 per day, discrimination between the income brackets was eliminated with about 30% of people signing up whether they were earning less than $25,000 per year or over $100,000 per year (see how the gap between the bars is eliminated on the right side of Figure 7.2).

The possibilities to help people through addressing individual behavioral differences and leveraging the digital world are vast. Whether it is trying to help workers in the Gig Economy (who may work in more precarious environments without safety nets), helping older generations work through complex problems associated with living in retirement, preventing the elderly from being preyed upon, or assisting people in making complex choices relative to healthcare and wellness, we can try to do more. It will take a mixture of setting the right goals, performing valuable research, getting the right mix of innovation, and performing testing. Goals. Research. Innovation. Testing. We can think of Behavioral GRIT™ to democratize outcomes.

Information Reframing Can Reduce Discrimination Between Income Brackets

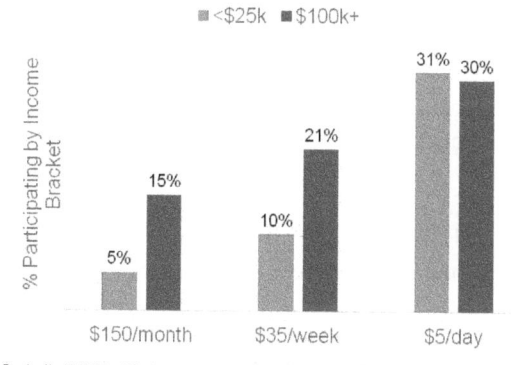

■ <$25k   ■ $100k+

Bracket	<$25k	$100k+
$150/month	5%	15%
$35/week	10%	21%
$5/day	31%	30%

Source: Based on Hershfield, Hal and Shu, Stephen and Benartzi, Shlomo. Temporal Reframing and Participation in a Savings Program: A Field Experiment (February 2, 2019). Available at SSRN: https://ssrn.com/abstract=3097468

Figure 7.2: Example of Democratizing Outcomes Through Nudging and Reducing Income Discrimination

Key Takeaways

Throughout this book, I've tried to address democratizing nudging in terms of how companies might try to implement behavioral science initiatives and how they might implement nudge units. However, in this chapter I've tried to explore a slightly different problem, which is about democratizing outcomes for end users. Here are some thoughts on how to think about this problem:

- **Try to define what it means to democratize outcomes** – This process might be messy and a tad philosophical, but it's important to think about goals (i.e., the "G" in GRIT) with an eye toward defining what it means to democratize outcomes. In some of the examples I've presented in this chapter, democratization is context-specific and includes things like helping those with lower numeracy, lower financial literacy, less income, and more occupational risk.

- **Consider individual behavioral differences in addition to traditional demographics** – Again, who we are can be just as important as what we are. Individual behavioral differences can include numerous things like loss aversion, myopia, positivity bias, self continuity, narrow framing, impatience, propensity to plan, risk aversion, ambiguity aversion, numeracy, financial literacy, need for control, etc. Prioritize potential scales or measures, perhaps in light of your definition of what it means to democratize outcomes. Consider subsampling some pertinent individual behavioral differences for subjects as part of your company's A/B tests. Analyze to what extent these factors influence people's decisions. Then consider whether there are possibilities to design choice environments to help people according to individual behavioral differences or to at least guard against undesirable discrimination.

- **Encourage behavioral science practices within your digital project teams** – There are many possibilities for achieving this. For example, you could establish a consulting office that works in conjunction with the digital teams. You could try to hire experts and try to locate them more closely within the product team. You could hire outsiders, such as consultants or academics who are well-versed in behavioral science and its applications. Other options include sending key employees to behavioral science training at a business school (e.g., executive or continuing education) or contracting for an in-house training workshop.

ACKNOWLEDGEMENTS

Thank you for reading *Nudging Democratized*. As I mentioned in the introduction, the application of behavioral science is in the early adoption phase. Many companies will benefit if they take time to develop the right approach. I hope this book can play a part in your journey.

Many thanks to my co-author, Andrew Lewis, for being a smart gentleman, terrific person to work with, and brilliant writer. Also, special thanks to Sekoul Krastev and Dan Pilat at The Decision Lab for making the publication possible and keeping things moving on this project.

Special thanks to my wife, Suzanne Shu, for supporting me in more ways than I could possible enumerate. I'd also like to thank my editor, Cynthia McIntyre for helping me with my writing projects. Thanks also to people like Kim Andranovich, Shlomo Benartzi, Linnea Gandhi, John Payne, Namika Sagara, and Cathy Smith for helping me shape my thoughts on various aspects of behavioral science. Finally in the interest of brevity, I'd like to thank numerous academics and clients who also influenced my thinking over the years.

I wish you the best of luck with implementing your behavioral science initiatives.

Best wishes and warmest regards,

Stephen Shu

BIBLIOGRAPHY

Allianz. http://knowledge.allianz.com/finance/behavioral_finance/?18 18/save-more-tomorrow-pension-savings-rates#popup-information-1994 (accessed July 8, 2015).

Allianz Global Investors. *About the Center - Center for Behavioral Finance.* http://befi.allianzgi.com/en/about-the-center/Pages/default.aspx (accessed June 16, 2015).

Allianz Global Investors Center for Behavioral Finance. *Introducing our New Book.* http://befi.allianzgi.com/en/save-more-tomorrow/Pages/key-themes-of-the-book (accessed June 15, 2015).

Allianz Global Investors Center for Behavioral Finance. *Retirement Goal Planning System.* May 27, 2015. https://itunes.apple.com/us/app/retirement-goal-planning-system/id921693236?mt=8 (accessed August 3, 2015).

Allianz Global Investors. *PlanSuccess Behavioral Audit Tool.* http://us.allianzgi.com/Retirement/BehavioralFinance/Pages/PlanSuccess.aspx (accessed June 16, 2015).

Ariely, Dan. *Predictably Irrational, Revised and Expanded Edition: The Hidden Forces That Shape Our Decision.* Harper Perennial, 2010.

Attali, Yigal, and Maya Bar-Hillel. "Guess Where: The Position of Correct Answers in Multiple-Choice Test Items as a Psychometric Variable." *Journal of Educational Measurement* 40, no. 2 (Summer 2003): 109-128.

Barstein, Fred. "The Future of DC Wholesaling." *NAPA Net the Magazine*, Spring 2015: 22-27, 42.

"Behavioral Insights Team Annual update 2010-11." *GOV.UK*. 2011. https://www.gov.uk/government/uploads/system/uploads/attachment_data/file/60537/Behaviour-Change-Insight-Team-Annual-Update_acc.pdf (accessed July 29, 2015).

Benartzi, Shlomo, Jonah Lehrer. *The Smarter Screen: Surprising ways to influence and improve online behavior.* Penguin, 2017.

Benartzi, Shlomo, and Roger Lewin. *Save More Tomorrow: Practical Behavioral Finance Solutions to Improve 401(k) Plans.* Portfolio, 2012.

Benartzi, Shlomo, and Roger Lewin. *Thinking Smarter: Seven Steps to Your Fulfilling Retirement.* New York: Penguin Publishing Group, 2015.

Blank, Steve. *Why Corporate Skunk Works Need to Die.* November 10, 2014. http://www.forbes.com/sites/steveblank/2014/11/10/whycorporateskunkworksneedtodie (accessed January 28, 2016).

Brosnan, Sarah, and Frans de Waal. "Monkeys reject unequal pay." *Nature* 425 (2003): 297-299.

Cialdini, Robert. "The Power of Social versus Economic and Regulatory Factors in Behavior Change." 2013. http://sites.nas.edu/socialandbehavioralsciences/files/2013/11/Cialdini_The-Power-of-Social-versus-Economic-and-Regulatory.pdf (accessed June 18, 2015).

Colquitt, Jason. "On the Dimensionality of Organizational Justice: A Construct Validation of a Measure." *Journal of Applied Psychology* 86, no. 3 (2001): 386-400.

Digitai. *Loss Aversion Calculator.* http://www.digitai.org/#lab (accessed August 3, 2015).

Farrell, Joseph. "Why OKCupid's 'Experiments' Were Worse Than Facebook's." *TheHuffingtonPost.com.* August 6, 2014. http://m.huffpost.com/us/entry/5655217 (accessed October 3, 2015).

FiduciaryFirst. *The Participant Effect.* http://fiduciaryfirst.com/participant-effect (accessed July 20, 2015) and updated based on correspondence with Jamie Hayes on October 20, 2015.

Fischhoff, B., et al. "Teen expectations for significant life events." *Public Opinion Quarterly* 64 (2000): 189-206.

Fung, Brian. "Facebook wants to know if you trust it. But it's keeping all the answers to itself." *The Washington Post.* December 31, 2013. https://www.washingtonpost.com/news/the-switch/wp/2013/12/31/facebook-wants-to-know-if-you-trust-it-but-its-keeping-all-the-answers-to-itself/ (accessed September 16, 2015).

Goel, Vindu. "Facebook Tinkers With Users' Emotions in News Feed Experiment, Stirring Outcry." *The New York Times*, June 29, 2014.

Goldstein, Daniel, Eric Johnson, Andreas Herrmann, and Mark Heitmann. "Nudge Your Customers Toward Better Choices." *Harvard Business Review*, December 2008.

Haidt, Jonathan. *The Righteous Mind: Why Good People Are Divided by Politics and Religion.* Vintage, 2013.

Halpern, David. *Inside the Nudge Unit: How Small Changes Can Make a Big Difference.* WH Allen, 2015.

Hershfield, Hal, et al. "Increasing Saving Behavior Through Age-Progressed Renderings of the Future Self." *Journal of Marketing Research* XLVIII (November 2011): S23-S37.

Hershfield, Hal, Stephen Shu, and Shlomo Benartzi. *Temporal Reframing and Participation in a Savings Program: A Field Experiment* (February 2, 2019). Available at SSRN: https://ssrn.com/abstract=3097468

Holmes, Thomas, and Richard Rahe. "The Social Readjustment Rating Scale." *Journal of Psychosomatic Research* 11 (1967): 213-218.

Hotten, Russell. "Volkswagen: The scandal explained." *BBC.* December 10, 2015. http://www.bbc.com/news/business-34324772 (accessed April 19, 2016).

ImpossibleObjects.com. *Coffeepot for Masochists.* http://impossibleobjects.com/catalogue/coffeepot-for-masochists.html (accessed July 27, 2015).

Iyengar, Sheena. *The Art of Choosing.* Twelve, 2011.

Johnson, Eric, and Dan Goldstein. "Do Defaults Save Lives?" *Science* 302 (November 2003): 1338-1339.

Kahneman, Daniel. *Thinking, Fast and Slow.* Farrar, Straus and Giroux, 2013.

Kahneman, Daniel, Jack Knetsch, and Richard Thaler. "Anomalies: The Endowment Effect, Loss Aversion, and Status Quo Bias." *The Journal of Economic Perspectives* 5, no. 1 (1991): 193-206.

Keeney, Ralph. *Value-Focused Thinking: A Path to Creative Decisionmaking.* Harvard University Press, 1996.

Kim, Susanna. "GymPact App Makes Workout Skippers Pay Up." *ABC News*. January 10, 2012. http://abcnews.go.com/blogs/business/2012/01/gympact-app-makes-workout-skippers-pay-up/ (accessed June 18, 2015).

Kim, W. Chan, and Renee Mauborgne. *Blue Ocean Strategy: How to Create Uncontested Market Space and Make Competition Irrelevant.* Harvard Business Review Press, 2005.

Kramer, Adam, Jamie Guillory, and Jeffrey Hancock. "Experimental evidence of massive-scale emotional contagion through social networks." *Proceedings of the National Academy of Sciences of the United States of America* 111, no. 24 (June 2014): 8788-8790.

Krishna, R. Jai. "Sandberg: Facebook Study Was 'Poorly Communicated'." *The Wall Street Journal.* July 2, 2014. http://blogs.wsj.com/digits/2014/07/02/facebooks-sandberg-apologizes-for-news-feed-experiment/?mod=LS1 (accessed October 3, 2015).

Leaf, Clifton. "Is Apple Watch a design flop?" *Fortune.com.* July 14, 2015. http://fortune.com/2015/07/14/design-apple-watch-wrong/ (accessed July 27, 2015).

Lockheed Martin Corporation. *Kelly's 14 Rules & Practices.* http://www.lockheedmartin.com/us/aeronautics/skunkworks/14rules.html (accessed January 29, 2016).

Lockheed Martin Corporation. *Skunk Works Origin Story.* http://www.lockheedmartin.com/us/aeronautics/skunkworks/origin.html (accessed January 29, 2016).

Ly, Kim, and Dilip Soman. *Nudging Around The World.* Research Report Series: Behavioral Economics in Action, Rotman School of Management, University of Toronto, 2013.

Mantonakis, Antonia, Pauline Rodero, Isabelle Lesschaeve, and Reid Hastie. "Order in Choice: Effects of Serial Position on Preferences." *Psychological Science* 20, no. 11 (2009): 1309-1312.

Martin, Roger. "The Price of Actionability." *Academy of Management Learning & Education* 11, no. 2 (2012): 293-299.

May, Matthew. *The Rules Of Successful Skunks Works Projects.* October 9, 2012. http://www.fastcompany.com/3001702/rulessuccessfulskunk worksprojects (accessed January 29, 2016).

McNaughton, Candace, Kerri Cavanaugh, Sunil Kripalani, Russell Rothman, and Kenneth Wallston. "Validation of a short, 3-item version of the subjective numeracy scale." *Medical Decision Making* 35, no. 8 (2015): 932-936.

Misbehaving Blog account on Twitter @MisbehavingBlog. June 18, 2015. https://twitter.com/misbehavingblog/status/61154508207701 6064?refsrc=email&s=11 (accessed June 19, 2015).

Mitchell, Deborah, J. Edward Russo, and Nancy Pennington. "Back to the Future: Temporal Perspective in the Explanation of Events." *Journal of Behavioral Decision Making* 2, no. 1 (1989): 25-38.

Norman, Donald. *The Design of Everyday Things revised and expanded edition.* The MIT Press, 2014.

Payne, John, James Bettman, and David Schkade. "Measuring Constructed Preferences: Towards a Building Code." *Journal of Risk and Uncertainty* 19, no. 1 (1999): 243-270.

Payne, John, Namika Sagara, Suzanne Shu, Kirstin Appelt, and Eric Johnson. "Life expectancy as a constructed belief: Evidence of a live-to or die-by framing effect." *Journal of Risk and Uncertainty* 46, no. 1 (February 2013): 27-50.

Pearce, Jone, and Laura Huang. "The Decreasing Value of Our Research to Management Education." *Academy of Management Learning and Education* 11, no. 2 (June 2012): 247-262.

Pratto, Felicia, Jim Sidanius, Lisa Stallworth, and Bertram Malle. "Social Dominance Orientation: A Personality Variable Predicting Social and Political Attitudes." *Journal of Personality and Social Psychology* 67, no. 4 (1994): 741-763.

Ries, Eric. *The Lean Startup: How Today's Entrepreneurs Use Continuous Innovation to Create Radically Successful Businesses.* Crown Business, 2011.

Rudder, Christian. "We Experiment On Human Beings!" *OkTrends.* July 28, 2014.

http://blog.okcupid.com/index.php/we-experiment-on-human-beings (accessed October 3, 2015).

Saghai, Yashar. "Salvaging the concept of nudge." *Journal of Medical Ethics* 39, no. 8 (2013): 487-493.

Salthouse, Timothy. "What and When of Cognitive Aging." *Current Directions in Psychological Science* (American Psychological Society) 13, no. 4 (2004): 140-144.

Seaman, Kendra, Mikella Green, Stephen Shu, and Gregory Samanez-Larkin. "Individual Differences in Loss Aversion and Preferences for Skewed Risks Across Adulthood." *Psychology and Aging*, 33, no. 4 (2018): 654-659.

Shankar, Maya. "Using Behavioral Science Insights to Make Government More Effective, Simpler, and More People-Friendly." *The White House: Office of Science and Technology Policy*. February 9, 2015. https://www.whitehouse.gov/blog/2015/02/09/using-behavioral-science-insights-make-government-more-effective-simpler-and-more-us (accessed July 29, 2015).

Shoven, John, and Sita Slavov. "Shoven-Slavov Retirement Booklet: Efficient Retirement Design." March 2013.

Shu, Suzanne, H. Min Bang, and Elke Weber. "Informed Consent to Choice Architecture: The Role of Transparency, Intention, and Perceived Effectiveness." Working Paper, August 2015.

Soman, Dilip. *The Last Mile: Creating Social and Economic Value from Behavioral Insights*. University of Toronto Press, 2015.

Sunstein, Cass. "Do People Like Nudges? (Preliminary Draft)." *Social Science Research Network*, July 2015.

Terwiesch, Christian, and Karl Ulrich. *Will Video Kill the Classroom Star? The Threat and Opportunity of Massively Open Online Courses for Full-Time MBA Programs*. Independent Report, Mack Institute for Technological Innovation at the Wharton School, University of Pennsylvania, 2014.

Thaler, Richard, and Cass Sunstein. *Nudge: Improving Decisions About Health, Wealth, and Happiness*. Yale University Press, 2008.

Thaler, Richard, and Shlomo Benartzi. "Save More Tomorrow: Using Behavioral Economics to Increase Employee Saving." *Journal of Political Economy* 112, no. 1 (2004): S164-S187.

Tversky, Amos, and Daniel Kahneman. "Judgment under Uncertainty: Heuristics and Biases." *Science* 185 (1974): 1124-1131.

Tversky, Amos, and Daniel Kahneman. "The Framing of Decisions and the Psychology of Choice." *Science*, 211, no. 4481 (January 1981): 453-458.

Unknown: Published by TVPUniversity. "Capuchin monkeys reject unequal pay." *YouTube*. December 15, 2012. https://youtu.be/lKhAd0Tyny0 (accessed October 3, 2015).

VanDerhei, Jack. "What Causes EBRI Retirement Readiness Ratings to Vary: Results from the 2014 Retirement Security Projection Model." *EBRI.org Issue Brief*, no. 396 (February 2014): 1-32.

Verganti, Roberto. *Design Driven Innovation: Changing the Rules of Competition by Radically Innovating What Things Mean.* Harvard Business Press, 2009.

Verma, Inder. "Editorial Expression of Concern and Correction." *Proceedings of the National Academy of Sciences of the United States of America* 111, no. 29 (July 2014): 10779.

Wohlsen, Marcus. "Know What You'll Look Like In 30 Years - Maybe Then You'll Max Out Your 401(k)." *Wired*. December 5, 2012. http://www.wired.com/2012/12/retirement-magic-mirror (accessed June 14, 2015).

Zaltman, Gerald, and Lindsay Zaltman. *Marketing Metaphoria: What Deep Metaphors Reveal About the Minds of Consumers.* Harvard Business Review Press , 2008.

APPENDIX A: IDEAS TO INTRODUCE BEHAVIORAL SCIENCE INITIATIVES

I wrote *Inside Nudging* to provide managers with a more detailed look at different perspectives related to behavioral science and its application in business. In this appendix[35], I provide both some ideas for introducing behavioral science initiatives and some jump-start things to think about.

First, a company needs to identify its goals and identify what type of **predominant organization model** it wants to pursue. If I were to make an analogy with food, think of the organization model as your main dish.

Second, a company should consider a number of **implementation elements** that may play a role during execution. Getting back to the food analogy, think of these elements as possible spices or options that you can (or sometimes should) add to your main dish.

---

[35] Special thanks to Namika Sagara (Behavioral Scientist and President, Sagara Consulting LLC at www.sagaraconsulting.com) and Suzanne Shu (Professor, UCLA Anderson School of Management at www.anderson.ucla.edu) for providing input and commenting on this appendix.

Predominant Organization Model

At a high-level, I've seen five predominant organization models that companies use to implement behavioral science. These are:
1. Innovation Center (focuses on broad integration into the business)
2. Thought Leadership Center (focuses on marketing and branding)
3. Internal Consulting Office (focuses on completing specific operational assignments)
4. Working Group / Steering Committee (focuses on developing cadence)
5. Ad-Hoc (informal or departmental use)

More details below, including some things to jump-start your thinking.

Predominant organization model	What it is	Things to think about
1. Innovation Center (focuses on broad integration into the business)	An organization dedicated to creating, co-creating, or reinventing products, services, tools, and content	• Identify your goals, and consider a holistic view. • Consider how research, innovation, and testing will work in concert. • Develop a vision, strategy, and multi-year plan.
2. Thought Leadership Center (focuses on marketing and branding)	An organization primarily dedicated to creating or co-creating content and channels for discussion (e.g.,	• Identify your goals, especially relative to marketing and branding. • While research may not need to be as extensive as with an Innovation Center,

		newsletters, whitepapers, media, forums)	consider what level of differentiation is desired. • Develop research, content development, and fact-checking capabilities that are appropriate to the approach.
3.	Internal Consulting Office (focuses on completing specific operational projects)	One or more resources that can provide support within the organization for behavioral science projects	• Consider the goals of the office with a particular eye toward the business case and realistic capacity of the office. • Determine what resources the office will provide versus the operating groups (with an eye toward research, innovation, and testing processes).
4.	Working Group / Steering Committee (focuses on developing cadence)	A group that meets regularly to identify goals, areas of interest related to behavioral science, areas to review, and actions to take	• Identify both business and science leader roles to establish the right alignment, priorities, and cadence for the group. • Potentially consider contracting with external resources to fill gaps on either an interim or more permanent basis.

5. Ad Hoc (informal or use at department level)	A situation where resources are spread out within an organization, such as in isolated pockets between different departments	• While ad hoc efforts can be both valuable and comfortable for an organization, consider investigating whether opportunities are being missed and whether actions should be taken.

Implementation Elements

Organizations use implementation elements to help strengthen their overall approach. There are at least eight key ones that I've run into:
- Advisory Board or Panel
- Science Bureau
- Behavioral Science Officer or Leader
- Testing Platform
- Blue Sky / Potential Initiatives
- Pilot Project
- Behavioral Audit
- Education Program

The sensibility of combining certain elements with specific organization models varies. For example, an advisory board and testing platform may be highly desirable for an Innovation Center, but these may be less desirable for a company choosing an Ad Hoc approach to behavioral science. Again, I include more details below, plus some things to jump-start your thinking.

Implementation elements	What it is	Things to think about
Advisory Board or Panel	Multiple, named experts that can provide broad and deep academic science, industry, and customer input from ideation through implementation	• Identify your organization's gaps in knowledge of behavioral science and the market. • Determine to what extent you can offer value to advisors (e.g., data for research, compensation, intangibles). • Develop formal documents covering purpose, structure, compensation, and other requirements.
Science Bureau	A somewhat loosely organized set of available experts (like a bullpen) that can provide academic support, generally in the form of talks or content	• Identify potential themes, venues, and experts to support the goals of your effort. • Given uncertainties associated with loosely organized efforts, think

		through potential upsides and downsides.
Behavioral Science Officer or Leader	A point person that provides vision and steering for scientific activities within the organization	• Identify a leader or potential person that can grow into the role. • Consider to what extent internal- or external-facing activities are expected. • Provide the leader with both enough room to operate and resources.
Testing Platform	Processes and capabilities to both A/B test (e.g., in the lab or field) and analyze results through statistical analysis	• If behavioral science efforts are to impact products or services, then testing capabilities need to be developed. • Testing capabilities will need to account for research, review board, test design, execution capabilities, participant recruitment, and analysis resources.

Blue Sky / Potential Initiatives	A clean slate that reflects a rethinking of what behavioral science possibilities an organization might pursue if resources were available	- Diversity and process are keys to blue sky thinking, so consider how ideas will be generated and the context (e.g., players, venues). - Figure out processes for elaborating on initiatives, developing thumbnail business cases, assessing complexity, prioritizing, allocating resources, etc.
Pilot Project	An effort to get started, test the market, and see the possibilities of executing future projects, recognizing that the organization is early in the learning curve	- While a strong project management discipline is required for a pilot, don't lose sight of any larger problem statements the organization may be trying to address (e.g., increasing know-how, strengthening innovation capability). - If a longer-term plan has not

		been developed, try to do so before the pilot ends.
Behavioral Audit	A behavioral science assessment of specific business elements, which may include products, services, communications, materials, websites, systems, and processes.	• The scope and depth of an audit is flexible, so revisit the problem statement that the business wants to address, and align the scope of the audit with the resources available. • Generally, behavioral audits should be conducted by behavioral science experts or people that have been trained.
Education Program	Materials, seminars, workshops, and courses on behavioral science and related topics	• Education programs may need to be tied in with other activities (e.g., product development, marketing, business development) in order to stick.

A downloadable version of the latest version of this appendix is available at www.InsideNudging.com.

PRAISE FOR INSIDE NUDGING

"Steve Shu's thoughtful and very readable book *Inside Nudging* provides a unique opportunity to understand how the research from behavioral science can be best exploited by business. While many popular books on behavioral science make a strong case for the value of the research, none have addressed how to exploit it in such a helpful and practical manner. A rarely mentioned secret brought into full view here is the fact that using behavioral science effectively is not so straightforward. Written specifically for business people and consultants Steve Shu shares his wide experience of consulting to explain the challenges and pitfalls of translating the ideas and findings of academic research into actionable solutions for real business problems. This book shows you how by giving examples of how real consultancy projects were shaped to deliver valuable results for working businesses. *Inside Nudging* acts as an intelligent interface between the ideas of the nerds in academia and the needs of real business people and offers tremendous potential for any business that needs to understand how people respond to their actions."
- Peter Ayton, Professor, Associate Dean of Research and Deputy Dean, Social Sciences, City University London

"Steve Shu has written an excellent book for companies looking to get started with behavioral economics. Through his use of case studies and actionable takeaways, he does a great job showing how decades of research can be combined with other business elements to accomplish amazing results. *Inside Nudging* is like an executive guidebook for practitioners."
- Dilip Soman, Professor and Corus Chair in Communications Strategy, Co-Director, Behavioural Economics in Action at Rotman (BEAR), Rotman School of Management, University of Toronto; Author of *The Last Mile*

"Based on the extensive experience as a management consultant specializing in incubating behavioral science initiatives, Steve offers one of the first books to discuss how business professionals can put behavioral science to use in their business settings. It's a must-read for any professionals interested in behavioral science initiatives at their organizations."
- Namika Sagara, Behavioral Scientist and President at Sagara Consulting LLC; Visiting Research Scholar at the Fuqua School of Business, Duke University

"Steve Shu has written an indispensable guide for any business person – or anyone working with business people – to build behavioral science capabilities within an organization. I have worked closely with Steve over the years and have always been impressed by his original thinking and problem-solving abilities. And now I am even more impressed by his ability to capture all his experience in such an intelligent, articulate guide book. It is simultaneously thoughtful, creative and eminently practical. It takes you step by step through the process, and guides you adeptly through key decisions that will be critical to your success. I wish I had had the benefit of this wonderful book when I was building a behavioral finance unit at the large financial services company where I formerly worked!"
- Cathy Smith, Principal, Digitai LLC; Former Director and Co-Founder for the Allianz Global Investors Center for Behavioral Finance

"*Inside Nudging* is a very readable, practical guide for professionals wanting to apply insights from behavioral economics to business and organizational settings. Steve provides a unique point of view as a business professional that actively works with well-known academics in the field."
- Terrance Odean, Rudd Family Foundation Professor of Finance, Haas School of Business, University of California, Berkeley

"With *Inside Nudging*, Steve has assembled a set of practical perspectives and frameworks for applying behavioral science within organizations. Complementing a growing popular literature on insights from this field, Steve's work contributes the structures – organizational, operational, and ethical – by which to actually deploy those insights in the real world."
- Linnea Gandhi, Managing Director at TGG Group and Laboratory Course Advisor at the University of Chicago Booth School of Business

"The field of behavioral economics is now at a point where dozens of interventions have been uncovered over the last several decades. Until now, no one has taken these insights and combined them in a practical, user-friendly way related to business. Steve Shu manages to accomplish just this task. Impressively, he does so in a way that stays true to the nuance of the original research studies, yet still makes behavioral economic considerations accessible and understandable."
- Hal E. Hershfield, Assistant Professor at UCLA Anderson School of Management

"This book makes the journey from exciting new ideas to making them work in practical settings. Behavioral science holds enormous promise for more effective and more enlightened strategies, but to realize the potential of behavioral science one needs to navigate many pitfalls and pay attention to the context in which ideas may be tried out. In this book Steve Shu helps the practitioner navigate the cliffs and keep an eye on the ultimate goal of successful implementation."
- Arie Kapteyn, Professor of Economics and Director of the Center for Economic and Social Research, University of Southern California

"Understanding how to use nudges effectively can dramatically improve managerial decision making, and I am delighted that Steve Shu has written an exciting new book for practitioners to help them on their way."
- Katherine L. Milkman, Associate Professor at the Wharton School of The University of Pennsylvania

ABOUT STEVE SHU

Steve Shu specializes in incubating new initiatives and business lines with a primary focus on services, technology, and behavioral science. He serves as a Managing Principal at Digitai, a behavioral economics consultancy and innovation firm. Steve has consulted to or had management roles at organizations such as The Voya Behavioral Finance Institute for Innovation, Allianz Global Investors Center for Behavioral Finance, Allscripts, Nortel Business Consulting, PRTM Management Consultants (acquired by PwC), and numerous startups. Steve is an advisor to The Decision Lab, and he is also an academic researcher at City, University of London, Cass Business School.

Steve holds an MBA from the University of Chicago and both an ME and BS in Electrical Engineering from Cornell University.

Steve has put his decades of experience into his solo-authored books, *Inside Nudging: Implementing Behavioral Science Initiatives* and *The Consulting Apprenticeship: 40 Jump-Start Ideas for You and Your Business*.

ABOUT ANDREW LEWIS

Andrew Lewis is a writer and behavioral scientist, focused on belief perseverance and how individuals evaluate new information. He is a PhD candidate in Politics at the University of Oxford, and a researcher at its Centre for Experimental Social Science (CESS). He was previously at Carnegie Mellon University, where he worked at the BEDR Policy Lab and Centre for Behavioral and Decision Research (CBDR), and was a research and teaching assistant to George Loewenstein. Andrew is editor-in-chief at The Decision Lab.

ABOUT THE DECISION LAB

The Decision Lab is a Canadian think-tank dedicated to democratizing behavioral science through research and analysis. We apply behavioral science to create social good in the public and private sectors. Since launching in 2013, we've become one of the leading publications in this space and have worked with organizations such as The World Bank, the Skoll Foundation and some of the largest financial institutions in Canada.

www.TheDecisionLab.com

Lightning Source UK Ltd.
Milton Keynes UK
UKHW051832121119
353397UK00012B/383/P